The
Anointed
& His
Anointing

Dag Heward-Mills

Parchment House

THE ANOINTED & HIS ANOINTING

First published 2016 by Parchment House
10th Printing 2017

"Find out more about Dag Heward Mills at:

Healing Jesus Campaign
Email: evangelist@daghewardmills.org
Website: www.daghewardmills.org
Facebook: Dag Heward-Mills
Twitter: @EvangelistDag

ISBN : 978-1-61395-558-1

Contents

Contents

CHAPTER 1

What Exactly is the Anointing?

> How God anointed Jesus of Nazareth with the Holy
> Ghost and with power: who went about doing good,
> and healing all that were oppressed of the devil; for
> God was with him.
>
> Acts 10:38

The anointing is the Holy Spirit. Every teaching you hear about the Holy Spirit is a teaching about the anointing.

The word "anointing" is both a verb and a noun. "Anointing" can mean the substance used to anoint a person; for example the anointing oil.

Anointing can also mean the act of pouring oil on someone.

When I speak of the anointing, I speak of the person of the Holy Spirit that is given to you to do the work of God. It is important to go beyond the anointed to see the anointing. The anointed is enveloped with the anointing of the Holy Spirit.

Jesus Christ of Nazareth went about doing good because He was anointed with the Holy Ghost and with power. Jesus could have been anointed with olive oil, engine oil, coconut oil or with Vaseline. If he had been anointed with any of these things we would safely say that the anointing substance is the olive oil, engine oil, coconut oil or Vaseline. But Jesus Christ was anointed with the Holy Spirit and power. We can therefore say that the anointing substance with which Jesus was anointed was the Holy Spirit. The mysterious Holy Spirit comes to abide upon a person who is anointed by God.

When a person is anointed, Almighty God moves to rest *upon* a person, *within* a person or to be *with* a person in a special way. This is what makes the person anointed and powerful. When you are dealing with an anointed person you are actually dealing with God. When you are dealing with an anointed person you are dealing with the Holy Spirit.

This is why there are such severe reactions to people who mishandle the anointed and his anointing. They are not actually mishandling men but they are mishandling God. When Ananias and Sapphira lied to Peter, who was anointed to be an apostle, they died instantly. This was a severe reaction which frightened the other church members. But Peter explained the mistake that Ananias and Sapphira had made. He said, "But Peter said, Ananias, why hath Satan filled thine heart to LIE TO THE HOLY

GHOST, and to keep back part of the price of the land? Whiles it remained, was it not thine own? And after it was sold, was it not in thine own power? why hast thou conceived this thing in thine heart? Thou hast not lied unto men, but unto God. And Ananias hearing these words fell down, and gave up the ghost: and great fear came on all them that heard these things" (Acts 5:3-5).

You see Ananias and Sapphira had actually lied to the Holy Spirit. They were not lying to Peter but to the Holy Spirit and that brings about severe and seemingly harsh responses. Be careful when you are dealing with anointed people. You may shorten your life and ministry because you underestimated and misjudged the greatness of the anointing they were carrying.

You may ask, "Why is it that many people lie to pastors today and do not seem to die instantly? Is it that they are not anointed?" The answer is simple. There are different types of manifestations of the Spirit at different times. Even in Peter's ministry, no one else died for telling lies. You can never tell when God's power will manifest in a certain way. I am sure many other people have died for telling lies to the Holy Spirit. It may not be instant death but death is still death.

CHAPTER 2

Where Exactly is
the Anointing?

The treasure of the anointing is found associated with the anointed. The anointing is inseparable from the man. The man of God has the anointing in him, with him or upon him.

Today, you and I are seeking for that which brings healing, breakthrough, deliverance and advancement in this life. It is the anointing! It is the anointing that breaks the yoke.

So where exactly is the anointing? Can we find the anointing in the West Hills Mall? Can we find the anointing in the West Gate Mall? Can we find the anointing in an office? Can we find the anointing at the airport? Can the anointing be found in a shop? No, the anointing is not in any of these places.

The anointing is found *IN* the anointed man!

The anointing is found *WITH* the anointed man!

The anointing is found *UPON* the anointed man!

The anointing is inseparable from the man whom God has anointed.

Which One Has the Power; the Anointing or the Anointed?

Since it is the anointing that really breaks the yoke, it is important to locate the anointing. Years ago, people discovered that oranges could cure diseases. After some time, science went further and discovered the element within the oranges that actually brought about the healing. They discovered Vitamin C! Today, many people simply focus on taking Vitamin C tablets. They have a revelation of the secret that brings the healing.

In the same way, there is an element in anointed men that performs wonders and that element is the anointing. Unfortunately, there is no chemical process to separate the anointing from the anointed man in the same way that Vitamin C has been separated from oranges. You are going to have to deal with the anointed man if you want to gain access to the anointing. There is simply no laboratory or factory that is producing real anointing in bottles which you can have without ever seeing the anointed man.

God has chosen a black man, a white man, an educated man or even an idiot to place His anointing upon. You are going to have to go to that person because he contains and carries the anointing. It is this lack of separation between the anointed and the anointing that is the undoing of proud Christians. "I want God to use me but I do not want to relate with His anointed to gain the anointing."

The Anointing in Three Places

1. The anointing is with an anointed person.

Even the Spirit of truth; whom the world cannot receive, because it seeth him not, neither knoweth him: but ye know him; FOR HE DWELLETH WITH YOU, and shall be in you.

John 14:17

5

2. The anointed carries the Spirit upon him.

The Spirit of the Lord *IS* UPON ME, because he hath anointed me to preach the gospel to the poor; he hath sent me to heal the brokenhearted, to preach deliverance to the captives, and recovering of sight to the blind, to set at liberty them that are bruised,

Luke 4:18

3. The anointed carries the Spirit within him.

But THE ANOINTING which ye have received of him ABIDETH IN YOU, and ye need not that any man teach you: but as the same anointing teacheth you of all things, and is truth, and is no lie, and even as it hath taught you, ye shall abide in him.

1 John 2:27

The anointing of the Holy Spirit is either in a person, with a person or upon a person. That is the exact location of the anointing. This is why an anointed man becomes important to you. He is the carrier of something that you need. He himself is weak, powerless, useless and human. But he has been chosen to carry a portion of the Spirit with him, in him or upon him. The anointing is so attached to the person and is so much a part of the person that we are often deluded into thinking that the person himself has some kind of power.

Your ability to handle the anointed and relate with the anointed person will determine your access to the anointing. Remember that it is the anointing you need. Just imagine you are longing for some orange juice in a jug. It is the orange juice that you need but you have to handle the jug with care because it is the jug that contains the orange juice.

Many people make spiritual mistakes when it comes to the anointed and his anointing. They want the anointing but they do not want anything to do with the anointed. They do not realise that their attitude towards the anointed human being is cutting them off from the anointing and leading to their downfall. God often anoints strange people and your ability to relate with strange, unusual or even odd personalities may be all that links you to the anointing.

In Psalm 89, you can learn about the dangers of mishandling the anointed who is carrying the anointing. God said, "I have found David my servant and with my holy oil have I anointed him." After declaring that He had anointed David He said, "My arm will strengthen him." Because David was anointed he was strong and undefeatable. The son of wickedness would not be able to afflict him because he was anointed. You cannot defeat an anointed person. God will crush you. You will fall and you will fail when you fight the anointed.

Those of you who choose to become enemies of anointed men must watch out because God said, "...I shall crush his adversaries before him, And strike those who hate him" (Psalm 89:23). Many people have shortened their lives and cut off their destinies because they have made themselves adversaries of anointed men.

There is even a curse for those who hate anointed people. He said, "...I will strike those who hate him', I will beat down his foes before his face and plague them that hate him" (Psalm 89:23). I would not like to be an enemy of the anointed.

It is time to recognize where the anointing resides. It is with the anointed, in the anointed and upon the anointed. That is why the clothes of an anointed person can also be anointed. This is why the woman with the issue of blood touched the hem of Jesus' garment and received a miracle.

The power of God is in the physical container whom we call the anointed. The anointed may be called a prophet, a pastor, a teacher, an apostle or even a brother. Like Jesus, he may not even have a title. But it is the anointing that breaks the yoke and makes the miracles happen for your breakthrough, your progress, your advancement and your deliverance in this life.

CHAPTER 3

How to Identify Anointed People

The greatest secret for your anointing is to identify the anointed who has been sent to you with his anointing. Remember that the anointed is an agent of God for your promotion, your deliverance and your lifting. Remember also that the anointed person is an agent for you to receive the anointing. To be able to do what an anointed person does, you must have his anointing. The reason why anointed people are able to do what they do is because of the anointing they have. You will also be able to do things that the anointed person has done if you can get his anointing.

It is therefore crucial for you to identify anointed people so that you can target the anointing that they carry.

How to Identify Anointed People

Today, people say that someone is anointed if he has a certain title. When a person is called Pastor, Prophet, Evangelist, Teacher or Apostle, it is usually assumed that he is anointed. Unfortunately, some people who are called Pastor, Prophet, Evangelist, Teacher and Apostle are not anointed. So how should anointed people be identified? Once again, the Bible will guide us in identifying anointed people.

1. Identify the anointed by the criteria of Jesus Christ.

The disciples of John the Baptist told John about everything Jesus was doing. So John called for two of his disciples, and he sent them to the Lord to ask him, "Are you the Messiah we've been expecting, or should we keep looking for someone else?"

Then he told John's disciples, "Go back to John and tell him what you have seen and heard - the blind see, the lame walk, the lepers are cured, the deaf hear, the dead are raised to life, and the Good News is preached to the poor. And tell him, 'God blesses those who do not turn away because of me.'"

Luke 7:18-19, 22-23 (NLT)

John the Baptist was a truly spiritual prophet. He wanted to know whether Jesus Christ was the famous anointed Messiah whom they were all expecting or not. Somehow, Jesus did not think it was necessary to give a simple answer like "Yes" or "No". Instead, He sent John a message describing His ministry achievement and works.

The achievements of Jesus Christ in which the blind saw, the lame walked, the deaf heard, and the dead were raised were unique achievements that could only be achieved by someone who was anointed by God.

The preaching of the gospel to the poor is also a special work of the ministry achieved only by truly anointed people. Ministers today measure themselves by the rich who attend their services. Indeed, it is always a pleasure for a pastor to have some rich people in his congregation. But it is a greater accomplishment to preach to the poor. Whom a person preaches to tells a lot about the kind of anointing he is carrying. Some people are more difficult to preach to. It is more difficult to sustain a ministry to the poor than it is to the rich. The fact that Jesus was preaching to the poor meant a lot to anyone who had ears to hear and eyes to see.

2. **Identify the anointed by the sign of "doing unusual things" with ease.**

There was a man of the Pharisees, named Nicodemus, a ruler of the Jews: The same came to Jesus by night, and said unto him, Rabbi, we know that thou art a teacher come from God: for no man can do these miracles that thou doest, except God be with him.

John 3:1-2

The kind of sign you are looking for is a sign of when somebody does something that is not natural, easy or usual to do. Parting the river Jordan is no ordinary feat. Nicodemus said to Jesus, "No one can do these things except God be with him." Sometimes, unbelievers are quick to identify the signs of an unusual person with unusual abilities whilst Christians stand by and hardly recognize the gift of God.

Watch people who have unusual abilities to preach and teach with ease. This unusual ability is a sign that should make you recognize the anointing. Watch those who can sing, compose songs, raise money, work with computers, manage people and do many other difficult tasks. The ease with which they accomplish these difficult tasks is a sign of the anointing on their lives. Andrae Crouch's ability to compose songs and dominate the Christian music scene for many years was a sure sign of the gift of God. You must be sensitive and notice the anointing as people carry out extremely difficult tasks like pastoring a church, evangelizing, healing the sick and ministering the Spirit with ease.

There are certain sure signs that a person is anointed. Sometimes there are signs that are given just for your benefit. When the fifty prophets saw how Elisha parted the river Jordan they knew that he was not an ordinary person any more. He was now *the anointed Elisha*. The sign of the Jordan being parted was given specially for the benefit of the fifty unanointed prophets who attended the prophets' school.

Elisha saw it and cried out, "My father! My father! I see the chariots and charioteers of Israel!" And as they disappeared from sight, Elisha tore his clothes in distress.

Elisha picked up Elijah's cloak, which had fallen when he was taken up. Then Elisha returned to the bank of the Jordan River. He struck the water with Elijah's cloak and cried out, "Where is the Lord, the God of Elijah?" Then the river divided, and Elisha went across. When the group of prophets from Jericho saw from a distance what happened, they exclaimed, "Elijah's spirit rests upon Elisha!" And they went to meet him and bowed to the ground before him.

2 Kings 2:12-15 (NLT)

But Jehoshaphat said, *Is there* not here a prophet of the LORD, that we may enquire of the LORD by him? And one of the king of Israel's servants answered and said, Here is Elisha the son of Shaphat, which poured water on the hands of Elijah.

2 Kings 3:11

3. Identify the anointed by the peculiarities of his life.

And his disciples asked him, saying, why then say the scribes that Elias must first come?
And Jesus answered and said unto them, Elias truly shall first come, and restore all things.

But I say unto you, that Elias is come already, and they knew him not, but have done unto him whatsoever they listed. Likewise shall also the Son of man suffer of them.

Then the disciples understood that he spake unto them of John the Baptist.

Matthew 17:10-13

Some anointed people have peculiar characteristics that are not necessarily ministry achievements. Both John the Baptist and Elijah had peculiar feeding and dressing habits which were not ministry achievements per se.

Interestingly, those peculiarities were signs of the anointing on their lives and Jesus used those peculiar signs to identify the spirit of Elijah on John the Baptist.

Jesus Christ clearly identified John the Baptist as someone who operated in the spirit and anointing of Elijah. The peculiarities of John the Baptist's ministry in which he lived and ministered in the desert, fed on locusts and wild honey, dressed in camel's hair and a leather belt, preached confrontational messages and challenged the king's wife were clear for everyone to see. But Jesus knew that it was a sign of the spirit of Elijah resting on John.

4. Identify the anointed by his inspirational prophesying.

But he that prophesieth speaketh unto men to edification, and exhortation, and comfort.

1 Corinthians 14:3

And when Paul had laid his hands upon them, the Holy Ghost came on them; and they spake with tongues, and prophesied.

Acts 19:6

And it shall come to pass in the last days, saith God, I will pour out of my Spirit upon all flesh: and your sons and your daughters shall prophesy, and your young men shall see visions, and your old men shall dream dreams:
And on my servants and on my handmaidens I will pour out in those days of my Spirit; and they shall prophesy:

Acts 2:17-18

Prophesying is one of the most immediate signs of the presence of the anointing. In the book of Acts, whenever people received the Holy Spirit's baptism they mostly spoke in tongues and prophesied. The speech, preaching and prophecies of a person are very important in identifying the anointing on a person's life.

If you are very sensitive and discerning, when you listen to a person preach, you will know whether they are anointed or not. I have watched many famous preachers and noticed the presence and sometimes the absence of the anointing.

Most people are just taken up by the shouting, the fanfare, the popularity and the celebrity status of the man of God. But none of these things guarantee the presence of the anointing.

5. Identify the anointed by his predictive prophesying.

Then Samuel took a vial of oil, and poured it upon his head, and kissed him, and said, *IS IT* NOT BECAUSE THE LORD HATH ANOINTED THEE *TO BE* CAPTAIN OVER HIS INHERITANCE?

And the Spirit of the LORD will come upon thee, and thou shalt prophesy with them, and shalt be turned into another man.

And let it be, when these signs are come unto thee, that thou do as occasion serve thee; for God *is* with thee.

And thou shalt go down before me to Gilgal; and, behold, I will come down unto thee, to offer burnt offerings, *and* to sacrifice sacrifices of peace offerings: seven days shalt thou tarry, till I come to thee, and shew thee what thou shalt do.

And it was so, that when he had turned his back to go from Samuel, God gave him another heart: and all those signs came to pass that day.

And when they came thither to the hill, behold, a company of prophets met him; and THE SPIRIT OF GOD CAME UPON HIM, AND HE PROPHESIED AMONG THEM.

And it came to pass, when all that knew him beforetime saw that, behold, he prophesied among the prophets, then the people said one to another, What *is* this *that* is come unto the son of Kish? *IS* SAUL ALSO AMONG THE PROPHETS?

1 Samuel 10:1, 6-10

When a person is anointed, he begins to have a prophetic and often predictive tone to his speech. The things that he says will start to happen and the things that he predicts often come to pass. The presence of the prophetic and predictive tone is often indicative of the anointing.

Another thing to look out for is the number of things the anointed person has said that have happened. I know a man of God who prophesied about his church building, that he would have fifty thousand members. At the time he prophesied he was renting a school hall and there was no way he could have had even a few thousand. Prophesying that you will seat fifty thousand members in your own building when you are renting a small school hall sounds ludicrous. Prophesying that you will have a church building which seats fifty thousand people when there is nothing like that in the whole world sounds like someone who is having delusions of grandeur.

But when these prophecies come to pass you are compelled to recognize the presence of a truly anointed person. It is important to notice the things that a person has predicted that have come to pass. Those are signs of a real prophet and a real anointing. That is how to recognize an anointed person. Don't bother yourself with titles. Do not bother yourself with which country a person comes from. Don't bother yourself with the colour of a person's skin. Look for real anointing on truly anointed people. When you have found an anointed person you have found a pearl of great value.

CHAPTER 4

It is the Anointing That Breaks the Yoke

And it shall come to pass in that day, *tha*t his burden shall be taken away from off thy shoulder, and his yoke from off thy neck, and the yoke shall be destroyed because of the anointing.

Isaiah 10:27

If any yokes will be broken, they will be broken by the anointing and not by the man of God. It is not the prophet that breaks the yoke! It is not the man of God that breaks the yoke! It is not the anointed pastor that breaks the yoke! It is not the anointed that breaks the yoke! It is the anointing that breaks the yoke! You must understand why miracles happen. You must understand how breakthroughs come about. It is the anointing that breaks all yokes. The yoke is destroyed because of the anointing and not because of the man.

There is nothing magical about a prophet, a pastor or a man of God. A man of God is a man. He has no powers of himself. I have seen the healing anointing operate in my ministry many times. But I myself have no powers to heal anyone. If you think a man of God has any power of himself you are well and truly deceived.

So how come a man of God is used to perform miracles, signs and wonders? Miracles, signs and wonders are a fruit of the anointing of the Holy Spirit. Scripture is clear: it is the anointing that breaks the yoke. If any yokes are broken, they are broken by the anointing and not by the man of God. You must therefore begin to see a man of God for what he really is: an anointed person carrying the anointing.

It is the anointing that works the miracles and not the title. Power does not rest in the title "Prophet". Power does not rest in the money, the car, the shouting, the style, the clothes or the dressing of the anointed man. Power rests in the anointing of the man of God who is carrying it.

If you, the man of God, think that you have any power to do anything, you are well and truly deceived. That was the deception that Lucifer had of himself! He was so shiny and so beautiful that he thought there was a light coming from within him. But there was no light coming from within Lucifer. All the glory and beauty that he had was from God's appointment and God's glory. God created him in splendour but he sinned by forgetting that he was a created and appointed being. A fire came from within him and destroyed him. No one has any power of himself. And a true man of God knows it. Look at how apostle Peter addressed those who thought he was powerful. "And when Peter saw it, he answered unto the people, Ye men of Israel, why marvel ye at this? Or why look ye so earnestly on us, AS THOUGH BY OUR OWN POWER OR HOLINESS WE HAD MADE THIS MAN TO WALK?" (Acts 3:12).

If there was any healing power belonging to any man of God, including myself, then we would be able to go to any hospital to heal and discharge everyone. Indeed there is no inherent power that a man of God or prophet possesses.

CHAPTER 5

The Anointing in the Field

Again, the kingdom of heaven is like unto TREASURE HID IN A FIELD; the which when a man hath found, he hideth, and for joy thereof goeth and selleth all that he hath, and buyeth that field.

Again, the kingdom of heaven is like unto a merchant man, seeking goodly pearls: Who, when he had found one pearl of great price, went and sold all that he had, and bought it.

Matthew 13:44-46

The anointing is the greatest treasure ever to be given to men. An anointed person is like a treasure hidden in a field. Unfortunately, this great treasure is hidden in the middle of a big field. You are going to have to pass through the gates or cross over the walls to gain access to the field.

You are going to have to wade through the streams in the field to gain access to the anointing. You are going to have to walk across the grass and the weeds to gain access to the treasure in the field. You are going to have to walk over the rocks to gain access to the treasure in the field. You are going to have to avoid the snakes to gain access to the treasure in the field.

People without energy have no time to cross the field to find the anointing. Lazy men cannot make the effort to wade through streams and carefully make their way over the grass and weeds in the field. If you have no time to search the field for this precious anointing, rest assured you will never have the anointing.

As you wade through the field, keep your eyes open for a man. This man will be carrying the anointing. It may be in him, it may be upon him or it may be with him. The treasure of the anointing is found upon the anointed. The anointing is inseparable from the man. The man of God has the anointing in him, with him or upon him.

It costs something to get near to the anointed person and to gain access to the anointing. Remember, it is the anointing you need, not the anointed. It is the anointing which breaks the yoke. It is not the anointed man who breaks the yoke but the anointing in him and the anointing upon him.

There is a price to pay to gain access to the anointing. Everyone who gains access to the anointing has paid the price. Jesus said, "Any man who comes after me must take up his cross and pay the price and follow me." To follow the anointed you will have to take up the cross that he carried.

James and John wanted to sit on the right hand of Jesus. Jesus simply asked a question, "...Are ye able to drink of the cup that

I shall drink of, and to be baptized with the baptism that I am baptized with?..." (Matthew 20:22).

The Price of the Anointing

1. **The cost of your time:** People who have no time to spare for the most important treasure will never receive it. Many people can spend hours watching television and listening to the news ten times a day. But these same people have no time to watch anointed videos. People spend hours on useless socialising but have no time to socialise with God. I sometimes marvel at people who are not prepared to wait to see the anointed and to interact with him. Only those who have made time and spent precious hours waiting for the anointed and his anointing are worthy to receive it. Are you prepared to pay the price and give quality time to the anointed for his anointing?

2. **The cost of humility:** People love the things that make them look great! If you are not prepared to part with what makes you great, you cannot have the anointing. I marvel at people who are not prepared to lower themselves and be subservient to an anointed person. Are you prepared to lower yourself and ask for prayer? Are you prepared to lower yourself and sit in a conference to learn what you do not know? Are you prepared to make yourself a servant to someone whom you once thought was an equal?

3. **The cost of openness:** People love their secrets! They do not want to part with their little secrets and their covered dignified life. It is wonderful how people come to the anointed and try to trick him, pretending to be humble servants and obedient followers. That is the spirit of Herod. It is the spirit of Herod which says, "Tell us where the king of glory is. I am also one of his worshippers", when in reality you are not one of his worshippers.

4. **The cost of learning new things:** People love to stick to what they learnt as children! It is a wonder to observe people who are not learning anything new and are not prepared to pay the price to learn new ways of doing ministry. Every new thing that must be learnt involves the pain and sacrifice of re-learning things. Sometimes the pain of learning to do new things is too much for people to go through.

5. **The cost of adjustment:** People love their old and traditional ways of doing things! It is marvellous to observe people who claim to want the anointing but who are not prepared to make any adjustments to their lives, their time, their schedule and their ways. The one who seeks the anointing is the one who must adjust his life to suit the anointed. The burden of adjustment is on the seeker. It is the one who is pursuing the anointing who has the burden of changing his lifestyle to accommodate the behaviour of the anointed.

6. **The cost of honour:** People are simply not prepared to pay the price to give real honour! It is fantastic to see people who want the anointing but will not pay the price to honour an anointed person. It costs time, money and effort to honour the anointed and his anointing.

Truly, the kingdom of Heaven is like a treasure which a man finds and pays the price to have the treasure.

7. **The cost of listening:** People do not listen to anointed men! It takes self-discipline to listen to the anointed. Talk less and listen more if you want to receive the anointing. You cannot receive the anointing unless you listen to the anointed. Jesus said, "The words I speak are Spirit and life." The words of the anointed contain the Spirit and the life that you need. Listen carefully when you are with the anointed. How can you receive the anointing if you never listen to messages, preaching and prophecies of the anointed?

CHAPTER 6

Unravel the Mystery of the Hidden Anointing

Again, the kingdom of heaven is like unto treasure **HID IN A FIELD**; the which when a man hath found, he hideth, and for joy thereof goeth and selleth all that he hath, and buyeth that field.

Matthew 13:44

Verily thou art a God that hidest thyself, O God of Israel, the Saviour.

Isaiah 45:15

If you have the boldness or energy to wade through the field, you are only halfway in the journey to the anointing. The anointing does not just lie openly in the field, otherwise most people would have just bought the field.

The anointing is a treasure that is actually hidden in a field. Most people have money in their houses. But hardly anyone leaves the money lying around in the open. Most people have hidden their money in their wardrobes or their drawers. Only a fool leaves his treasure lying around as though it has no value. The cities of London, Paris and New York have much more treasure than cities in certain poor countries. But if you walk on the streets of London, Paris and New York, you will not find any more treasure lying about than if you were to walk on the streets of poorer countries. The great treasures and the great wealth of London, Paris and New York are in London, Paris and New York, but they are hidden. You are near the treasure but you cannot see it because it is hidden. Once you get into the field, you are near the treasure but it does not lie about in the open. It is not obvious. There is still a mystery to solve. This is why you must unravel the mystery of anointed people. If you are able to decipher or understand them, you will gain access to the great treasure that is hidden in them.

In this chapter, the emphasis is on the word "hidden". The treasure of God is intentionally concealed so as to keep away casual browsers and unserious seekers. The anointing is the treasure that is hidden in the field. Anointing is hidden within or upon the anointed. Therefore, you will have to unravel any mysteries that the anointed person presents to you. Anointed people are often strange, unusual and not easy to read. If you think you know everything about the anointed, you probably know the least of all.

Behold, I go forward, but he is not there; and backward, but I cannot perceive him: On the left hand, where he doth work, but I cannot behold him: he hideth himself on the right hand, that I cannot see him:

But he knoweth the way that I take: when he hath tried me, I shall come forth as gold.

Job 23:8-10

Think about the anointed people in the Bible - Moses, David, Elijah and Elisha. There are so many oddities about each of the people that God used. Moses was Egyptian-trained with a foreign wife. David was a shepherd boy, unwanted by his family. David was a fighter and warrior who killed bears and lions for his pastime and sang psalms whilst he did so. Elijah was a strange and mysterious man who lived in the desert, like a wild animal, only appearing when it was time to give a prophecy, slipping back into the darkness when he had finished. Elisha was even stranger because he had twice the anointing on Elijah's life.

John the Baptist came along fasting and living in the desert, dressed in a funny way, eating strange things and running a church in the worst possible location for church growth. Jesus Christ, the anointed Saviour was the opposite. He came along eating, drinking and visiting the worst known sinners in town. Most of the people who have carried the anointing were not easy to read or understand. Why is this?

The kingdom of God is a like a treasure hidden in a field. The kingdom of God is not available for casual browsers but for deep-searching individuals who really want the treasure. The treasure will not be found by the proud and presumptuous who are too big to look further and to search harder.

The treasure of the anointing is not available for those who are dissuaded or distracted by the appearance and oddities of the anointed. God has no apologies for where He has placed His anointing. Most of the time, He places His anointing in an unusual spot and only real seekers will find it.

People who cannot wait, people who cannot search, people who are easily offended and people who are easily put off are all left out because the anointing is hidden from them. There are times God has hidden His gift in people with obvious sin. Moses the murderer and David the adulterer are clear examples of this. There are times that God has hidden his anointing in social misfits and deviants. Elijah is an example of this. There are times that God had hidden his anointing in people without protocol. John the Baptist is a good example of such people. There are times that God has hidden his anointing in the backslidden. Without the ability to relate to and respect a backslidden king like Saul, you will miss the anointing. The anointing keeps being passed on to outsiders and unexpected candidates because it is hidden from the view of proud people. Could it be that you are missing the anointing because you cannot see or imagine God using somebody who does things differently from the way you would expect things to be? But that is what hides the anointing from you.

There are many people who have been baffled by the way I operate in the anointing. They expected me to do things in a certain way. Many people have expected me to be a certain colour, speak with a certain accent, dress in a certain way, drive a certain type of car and live in a certain kind of area. When I do not meet these expectations, they get cut off from the anointing. But the anointing is intentionally hidden, so that only the humble can discover it.

Even in the natural, gold is obtained by those who are prepared to dig deep and go hundreds of feet below the earth to find the treasure. Oil, which is black gold, is also found deep within the earth and reserved for treasure hunters who are prepared to pay the price to live on the sea and do all sorts of strange things to get it.

Such is the nature of great treasure. Great treasures are always hidden. Even your little treasures are hidden away in a bank. No one puts his life's savings on a plate in front of the gate. God has equally hidden His best treasure, the anointing of the Holy Spirit deep within the anointed. You are going to have to manoeuvre through the nationality, the colour, the personality, the accent, the education, the culture and the background of a man in order to gain access to the anointing. If the anointing is found in an American or a Nigerian and you hate either of these two countries you will miss the anointing. Remember, the anointing is found in the anointed or upon the anointed!

CHAPTER 7

The Voice of the Anointed

And after six days Jesus taketh Peter, James, and John his brother, and bringeth them up into an high mountain apart,

And was transfigured before them: and his face did shine as the sun, and his raiment was white as the light. And, behold, there appeared unto them Moses and Elias talking with him.

Then answered Peter, and said unto Jesus, Lord, it is good for us to be here: if thou wilt, let us make here three tabernacles; one for thee, and one for Moses, and one for Elias.

While he yet spake, behold, a bright cloud overshadowed them: and behold a voice out of the cloud, which said, This is my beloved Son, in whom I am well pleased; HEAR YE HIM.

And when the disciples heard it, they fell on their face, and were sore afraid.

Matthew 17:1-6

G od will go to great lengths to make you to listen to the anointed, because of the anointing he is carrying. Almighty God went to great lengths to make the disciples listen to the voice of Jesus the Anointed Saviour. The whole transfiguration experience was simply to get the disciples to listen to the voice of Jesus. The only message that came to the disciples was "Hear ye him!" Hear ye him! Listen to him! Listen to his voice! Hearing a voice can change your life!

It is important for you to develop a culture for hearing the voice of the anointed. You can have the sound of the anointed with his anointing all the time. The disciples were taken all the way to the top of the mountain for them to know that they should listen to Jesus. *don't be full too quickly, feed like an elephant (16 hours)*

To be anointed is far different from being appointed. What we need is the anointing, not the appointment. You can be appointed but not anointed. When people aim for the appointment, they stop listening to the anointed and then they lose the connection to the anointed and his anointing by their disobedience.

Aim for the *anointment* and not the appointment! The anointing is what will make room for you. If you want to walk in the anointing, you must listen to/hear the anointed for years.

The anointed is in your life with his anointing when you are listening to him. The closer you are to the anointed, the more pieces of anointing will drop on you.

The Blessedness of the Anointed Voice

1. **The voice of the anointed carries honour and glory for you.**

   For he received from God the Father honour and glory, when THERE CAME SUCH A VOICE TO HIM FROM THE EXCELLENT GLORY, This is my beloved Son, in whom I am well pleased.

   2 Peter 1:17

You'll be honoured,
Beautiful and attractive.
Be connected to the anointed to get ~~easy~~ glory.

Jesus Christ received honour and glory when there came to him a voice from the excellent glory. Do you not want to receive honour and glory in your ministry? Jesus Christ received honour and glory when this great voice came to Him from the excellent glory. Hearing the voice of God will make all the difference to your ministry. Hearing an anointed voice can equally have great impact on your life and ministry. Why would hearing the voice of a man have any impact on another man? It is because God also speaks by His prophets and anointed men. He actually uses them to speak.

> **I HAVE ALSO SPOKEN BY THE PROPHETS, and I have multiplied visions, and used similitudes, by the ministry of the prophets... And by a prophet the LORD brought Israel out of Egypt, and by a prophet was he preserved.**
>
> **Hosea 12:10, 13**

Be alert, attentive, aware, keep an eye on, take heed.

From today, you must watch out for the voice of the anointed person. God is also speaking by these prophets. Carefully and cautiously handle the preaching, speaking, chatting and conversations of the anointed. Most of the famous teachings of Jesus came from His discussions with the disciples

The voice of the anointed carries the blessing of God. As you expose yourself to the voice of the anointed, you can expect honour and glory to be imparted into your ministry. All preachers who do not expose themselves to the anointed voice are missing out on the honour and glory that they could have received on their lives and ministry. And that is why you must expose yourself to it carefully.

2. The voice of the anointed carries the gift of the Spirit.

There is an impartation of gift to teach etc.

> **And the spirit entered into me when he spake unto me, and set me upon my feet, that I heard him that spake unto me.**
>
> **Ezekiel 2:2**

It's not just writing what he says.
When you listen, a gift is imparted.
— teach, outreach, pastor, lead,

29

Don't rush to repreach & message. Listen to it again and again.

While Peter yet spake these words, the Holy Ghost fell on all THEM WHICH HEARD THE WORD.

                                                    Acts 10:44

The voice of the anointed will bring you to the gift of the Holy Spirit. Ezekiel received the spirit when the voice spoke to him. The house of Cornelius received the Holy Spirit when Peter preached to them. As they listened to the voice of Peter the Spirit descended on them. This is what happened to me in 1988 whilst I listened to the anointed voice of Kenneth Hagin. As I listened to his voice the Spirit entered into me and I became anointed to teach and to preach. I heard a voice coming to me and saying, "From today you can teach." Through that anointing to teach and preach, I have written several books.

Your personality can be affected too.

3. The voice of the anointed carries promotion.

And it shall come to pass, if thou shalt HEARKEN DILIGENTLY UNTO THE VOICE of the Lord thy God, to observe and to do all his commandments which I command thee this day, that the Lord thy God will set thee on high above all nations of the earth:

                                                    Deuteronomy 28:1

After the journey of the Israelites through the wilderness, God asked Moses and the Israelites to listen to His voice. He promised them that listening to his voice would guarantee them being lifted to a higher level, above the nations that had surrounded them. All your promotion in the ministry depends on your ability to hear and obey the voice of God.

4. The voice of the anointed carries establishment for you.

And they rose early in the morning, and went forth into the wilderness of Tekoa: and as they went forth, Jehoshaphat stood and said, HEAR ME, O JUDAH, and ye inhabitants of Jerusalem; Believe in the LORD your God, SO SHALL YE BE ESTABLISHED; believe his prophets, so shall ye prosper."

                                                    2 Chronicles 20:20

The voice of the anointed prophet brought establishment to king Jehoshaphat as he listened to and obeyed the voice of the prophet. You will need a push forward in your life and ministry. This forward push will come to you through the voice of the anointed. The voice of the anointed carries the spirit of counsel and direction that will lead to your establishment.

Jehoshaphat was faced with a very difficult situation. Several kings were about to attack him and his nation was in crisis. He had called for a prayer meeting; much prayer had been offered to the Lord. At the end of the prayer meeting, one of the pastors, Jahaziel gave a prophecy. He prophesied that they were going to win the war. He predicted that God was going to fight for them and that everything was going to be okay.

Jehoshaphat, a church member, exhorted the rest of the congregation to believe in God as well as God's anointed men. This famous speech teaches us a very great lesson. The first lesson is that believing in God will lead to establishment. The second lesson is that believing in the prophet will lead to prosperity.

Because of his great faith in the man of God, Jehosophat made the choir march out in front of the army. That was a very dangerous move! But he believed in both God and the prophet – and it paid off! At the end of it all, Jehoshaphat and his followers had more blessings than they could carry away. God blessed them with more than they could carry!

And when Jehoshaphat and his people came to take away the spoil of them, they found among them in abundance both riches with the dead bodies, and precious jewels, which they stripped off for themselves, MORE THAN THEY COULD CARRY AWAY: and they were three days in gathering of the spoil, it was so much.

2 Chronicles 20:25

The Hebrew word translated "established" in 2 Chronicles 20:20 is the word "Aman". It means "to nurture", "to foster as a

31

parent", "to build up" and "to nurse". This teaches us that as you believe in God, you will be nurtured and nursed by God. He will build you up in the faith and you will receive a strong foundation that only a parent can give.

But the Scripture also teaches that when you believe in the prophets you will "prosper". The Hebrew word translated "prosper" is the word "Tsalach." It means "to push forward", "to go over", "to come mightily" and "to break out!" "Aman" and "Tsalach" are two very different experiences. Being nurtured and having a mighty breakthrough in your life are two very different experiences.

God will nurture you and build you up. He will nurse you like a baby in a cradle. He will foster you like a parent and encourage you until you are well developed. But you will need a push forward in life. You need to break through mightily in this life. You need to break out into the fullness of your calling. God wants you to go over every wall and obstacle in your life.

The question is, "How will you receive this push forward in life?" After you have been nurtured and fostered by Almighty God, what is the key to coming mightily to the front in life? The key is to believe in the man of God.

Some people have difficulty in believing in the man of God. They say, "I can believe in God, but I can't trust these men." They say, "I cannot put my trust in the arm of flesh." What you must realize is that you are not putting your trust in a human being per se. You are supposed to believe both in God and in the man of God. One without the other will not get you where you need to go.

Believing in God without believing in his prophets will help you to be nicely built up in Christ. But you will not have the push forward that you need. Believing in the man of God without believing in God is also very dangerous! You could easily make a mistake and follow the errors of a human being. That is why the two go together!

All through the Bible, you are encouraged to believe in God and also to believe in His servants, the anointed ones. God hardly does anything without using these anointed people. He anointed them for that purpose and raised them up to speak His words. They are not words of mere men. They are words from above.

5. The voice of the anointed carries doctrine, correction, reproof and instruction.

For the prophecy came not in old time by the will of man: but holy men of God spake as they were moved by the Holy Ghost.

2 Peter 1:21

All Scripture is given by inspiration of God, and is profitable for doctrine, for reproof, for correction, for instruction in righteousness:

2 Timothy 3:16

The voice of the anointed carries the Scripture. As the voice carrying the Scripture comes to you, you will receive instructions, reproof, correction and doctrine. The Scripture is equally a prophecy and is heavily anointed. As you receive the voice that carries the Scripture, expect to receive instruction, reproof and great wisdom for your life.

- Your church has not been growing because you have not swallowed enough anointing to grow a church.
- Everything by the anointing.
You not doing outreaches co2 u don't have ē anointing.
Anything you see map it to the anointing. even small boys.
The manifestation of Eph 4:11 is in a pastor.
- What do u need from the person you are following.

33

CHAPTER 8

What It Means to Believe His Prophets

And they rose early in the morning, and went forth into the wilderness of Tekoa: and as they went forth, Jehoshaphat stood and said, Hear me, O Judah, and ye inhabitants of Jerusalem; Believe in the Lord your God, so shall ye be established; BELIEVE HIS PROPHETS, SO SHALL YE PROSPER.

2 Chronicles 20:20

This beautiful Scripture teaches us that believing in the prophet of God is important. Believing in God is important, but it is difficult to believe in God without believing in His prophets. Indeed, believing in God without believing in His prophets will not get you very far. God has mysteriously linked your prosperity, advancement and pushing forward in the ministry to your ability to believe in His prophets.

1. **"Believe his prophets, so shall ye prosper" is to give equal energy for your belief in God as well as for your belief in the prophets.**

Believing in God is important. Believing in the anointed man is also important. No one has successfully received from God without believing in the prophet of God.

The whole world cannot be saved without believing in Jesus.

The Israelites could not be saved without accepting Moses.

Jehoshaphat knew that their deliverance depended on believing in God as well as believing in the prophet.

Jesus said, "Believe in God, believe also in me."

So what exactly does it mean for you to believe in His prophets?

And they rose early in the morning, and went forth into the wilderness of Tekoa: and as they went forth, Jehoshaphat stood and said, Hear me, O Judah, and ye inhabitants of Jerusalem; Believe in the Lord your God, so shall ye be established; believe his prophets, so shall ye prosper.

2 Chronicles 20:20

2. **"Believe his prophets, so shall ye prosper" is to receive the man who is a prophet.**

Receiving the man of God is as important as believing in him. Without receiving the person you cannot really say that you believe in his words. You cannot reject the person and expect

35

to receive the anointing. You have to receive him if you want to enjoy what he is carrying.

> **But as many as received Him, to them He gave the right to become children of God, even to those who believe in His name.**
>
>

John 1:12, NASB

3. "Believe his prophets, so shall ye prosper" is to move away from trying to understand the prophets.

Believing things is different from understanding things. Believing in the gift and the anointing is more important than understanding it. You cannot wait till you understand how a car is made before you start driving one.

Many people want to understand what is happening before they fully commit themselves and believe fully. If you are going to wait to understand how a mobile phone works before you use one, I assure you that you will be left out of many things. It is time to grow up spiritually and believe faster than you understand.

4. "Believe his prophets, so shall ye prosper" is to obey the prophets.

Believing in the anointed is shown by your obedience to the anointed. It is this obedience that draws more of the gift from the anointed person! When you do not obey the anointed, it means you do not believe in his anointing.

When you obey someone you make a connection with the person and you are drawn to the person!

The anointed and his anointing are drawn towards people who obey his words. Your disconnection from the anointed is because of your disobedience to his words and prophecies.

The more you obey someone, the more you demonstrate your belief for the person. The more you believe and the more you obey, the more you love a person. Jesus clearly promised that He would manifest Himself towards those who obey Him.

Obedience is the sign of your love and it provokes the anointing. There will be no manifestation towards those who do not obey.

"He that hath my commandments, and keepeth them, he it is that loveth me: and he that loveth me shall be loved of my Father, and I will love him, and will manifest myself to him. Judas saith unto him, not Iscariot, Lord, how is it that thou wilt manifest thyself unto us, and not unto the world? Jesus answered and said unto him, If a man love me, he will keep my words: and my Father will love him, and we will come unto him, and make our abode with him. He that loveth me not keepeth not my sayings: and the word which ye hear is not mine, but the Father's which sent me. These things have I spoken unto you, being yet present with you" (John 14:21-25).

5. "Believe his prophets, so shall ye prosper" is to follow the detailed instructions of the anointed.

There are times the anointed will pass on detailed instructions to you. The power of God will work in your life as you follow these instructions. Anyone who is experienced with the anointed will take heed when specific instructions come forth from the anointed. Mary, the mother of Jesus, told the people to do whatever Jesus told them. "His mother saith unto the servants, Whatsoever he saith unto you, do it" (John 2:5).

Naaman was told to go and wash seven times. Not a word more! If you do not follow the instructions of the anointed you will not benefit from his anointing.

So Naaman came with his horses and with his chariot, and stood at the door of the house of Elisha.

And Elisha sent a messenger unto him, saying, Go and wash in Jordan seven times, and thy flesh shall come again to thee, and thou salt be clean.

2 Kings 5:9-10

CHAPTER 9

Receive the Anointed According to His True Rank

He that receiveth a prophet in the name of a prophet shall receive a prophet's reward; and he that receiveth a righteous man in the name of a righteous man shall receive a righteous man's reward.

Matthew 10:41

To receive the prophet in the name of a prophet is to receive the man of God in his proper rank. Every man of God is many things in one. He may be a father, a friend, a pastor, a prophet, a businessman, a leader, a relative or even an apostle. What do you receive him as?

If I am a medical doctor but you see me as a herbalist, you will not be open to my medical practice. You will not comply with the things I say or the things I do. You will not receive the benefits that you could have received from a real medical doctor from me.

In my experience as a man of God, I have discovered that people receive me in different ways. Some people receive me as a friend. Others receive me as a good leader. Some receive me as a lucky person who has had a good amount of success. Others receive me as a black man and some as a white man. Depending on how they receive me, a certain anointing flows to their lives. Some receive me as a pastor, whilst others receive me as a prophet.

I have never seen those who receive me as a relative being blessed by my prophetic ministry. I have never seen those who think of me as a lucky or successful person being blessed by my apostolic or pastoral ministry. And I have never seen those who see me as a pastor being blessed by the prophetic anointing on my life. If you see someone as "high up", "high up" things will come to you. If you regard someone as nothing, you will receive nothing.

I once worked with some Christians who did not know that I was a music producer and director. They received me as an outdated, defunct pianist who could only remember a few of his favourite songs from another era. That is exactly what they got from me. They received the rewards and benefits that you can get from an outdated, outmoded, musician. Some years later, I met other Christians who received me as a music director and supervisor. They received the benefits that came from having a great music director. Soon, they were famous artistes with worldwide acclaim.

What does this all mean? It means you must study the anointed carefully and recognize the true status of the person you are dealing with. How high up the ladder is he? What kind of power and grace is upon his life?

There are many times I have noted certain thoughts that came to my heart about certain men of God. Once, I was musing about a man of God who went around preaching the gospel of Jesus Christ. As I analysed his ministry, I realized that there were many nations that would give him a tumultuous welcome and receive him as though they were receiving Christ himself. I realized that there were few ministers of the gospel who were so widely known and who would be received by entire nations. These thoughts had come to my mind so that I would recognize the kind of rank I was dealing with and the level of anointing in that man of God.

On another occasion, I was musing about the ministry of another great man of God. I realized that he had given birth to a huge denomination that was affecting Africa. There was hardly any African nation I would go to where I would not see his church growing prominently and dominating the capital city. I realized that he was a very great apostle. These thoughts came to my mind because God wanted me to recognize the kind of apostle he was.

One day, whilst visiting a huge church, I watched a documentary about the pastor and his ministry. The Holy Spirit whispered to me that I did not know the extent of the greatness of the pastor of that church. The Holy Spirit whispered to my heart asking how many pastors can fill an Olympic Stadium at eight o'clock on Monday morning in a busy city of the world? Very few people can do such things!

As long as you see a person in a certain way, you receive a corresponding reward. If I am a great prophet but you see me as a minor prophet, I will be a minor prophet to you. You must study anointed people and recognize the true greatness of their rank.

CHAPTER 10

Walk in the Blessedness of Transference of Spirits

To walk in the blessedness of the transference of spirits, you must respect anointed men because they are carrying the anointing that you want to be transferred to you. You must therefore deal with God but also carefully handle the man who is anointed because he is carrying the anointing. There are fools who think they are just dealing with God and so they can mistreat the anointed man. Read your Bible carefully and you will find out that no one ever became anointed by God until he related properly with the anointed person. Many of those who have quarrelled with their spiritual fathers and mentors are never able to receive the anointing they desire. They pray to God all right but they fight the fathers and mentors God gives to them.

Read your Bible carefully and you will see that when God decides to give you His anointing, He will direct you to an anointed person.

It is true that this good and perfect gift is coming from above. But God has chosen to place His mantle on human beings. God does not seem to want to create a new anointing, but rather to share, re-distribute, pass on and divide anointings that He has already placed on people. Even John the Baptist was using an old anointing of Elijah. The two prophets in the book of Revelation will be carrying the anointing of Moses and Elijah. You cannot escape the reality that God does not readily introduce a new anointing.

God is the initiator of the transference of spirits. It is God who gives people the gifts and the ministries they have. Sometimes, people seek the anointing as though it is something they can force on themselves. You cannot engineer the anointing and you cannot shout it into existence. Wearing an anointed person's clothes, serving him, giving him offerings and hands being laid on you will not guarantee that you will catch the anointing.

It was God who took the anointing that was on Moses and put it on the seventy elders. It was not Moses who took his anointing and put it on the seventy elders. It was not the seventy elders who took the anointing that was on Moses and put it on themselves. God is the one who takes the anointing and places it on someone else.

And Moses went out, and told the people the words of the Lord, and gathered the seventy men of the elders of the people, and set them round about the tabernacle.

And THE LORD CAME DOWN in a cloud, and spake unto him, AND TOOK OF THE SPIRIT that *was* upon him, and GAVE IT UNTO THE SEVENTY elders: and it came to pass, *that*, when the spirit rested upon them, they prophesied, and did not cease.

Numbers 11:24-25

Because of this, your prayers must be directed to God and not to the anointed. You cannot pray to an anointed person or worship an anointed person. He is just carrying a gift which he did not engineer or conjure up. Anointed people may not even know that they are anointed.

Another important Scripture you must bear in mind is that "A man can have nothing except it is given to him from above."

John answered and said, A man can receive nothing, except it be given him from heaven.

John 3:27

This is an eternal principle. You can only have what God has given to you. This is the reason to even fear, respect and revere anointed people. Why did God give this person so much anointing? Why did God choose this person? Why did God bestow his love and gift on this particular person? God's choice should make you wonder and fear. That is why He says, "Touch not mine anointed." (Psalm 105:15). Most of the time we do not know why God anoints and chooses certain people. But always remember that the anointed person would have had nothing unless God had given it to him.

Every good gift and every perfect gift is from above, and cometh down from the Father of lights, with whom is no variableness, neither shadow of turning.

James 1:17

The anointing is also a good and perfect gift. What is more perfect than the gift of the Holy Spirit?

The Holy Spirit is the most wonderful gift God the Father can bestow on you or me. This good and perfect gift does not and cannot come from any man on this earth. I would advise you to seek God for this wonderful and perfect gift. This truth is a reality that multiplies the mysticism around the anointing. The anointing is given by God but it is found on the anointed, in the anointed and with the anointed person.

CHAPTER 11

The Mystery of Impartation

For God is my witness, whom I serve with my spirit in the gospel of his Son, that without ceasing I make mention of you always in my prayers; Making request, if by any means now at length I might have a prosperous journey by the will of God to come unto you.

For I LONG TO SEE YOU, THAT I MAY IMPART UNTO YOU SOME SPIRITUAL GIFT, to the end ye may be established; That is, that I may be comforted together with you by the mutual faith both of you and me.

Now I would not have you ignorant, brethren, that oftentimes I purposed to come unto you, (but was let hitherto,) that I might have some fruit among you also, even as among other Gentiles.

Romans 1:9-13

The mystery of impartation occurs in three dimensions: hearing, seeing and touching. This is why Paul longed to see the Romans. He knew that the mystery of impartation would be activated when he actually saw them and interacted with them. When you see someone, three things become possible: seeing, hearing and touching. Through the mystery and blessedness of seeing, hearing and touching, an anointing, a gift, a spiritual blessing can be imparted to you.

Today, through the witty inventions of modern technology, two of these three blessings are possible. Seeing and hearing is possible through audio and video devices. Through technology, you can receive an impartation from someone whom you do not even physically see. Through technology, you can be anointed by just listening to audio messages. This is because the essential elements in the mystery of impartation are fulfilled. Even with the death of the anointed, you can still hear his voice and watch him minister. I have videos of many anointed men who have died and passed on. Their lives are a great blessing to me and I am always receiving impartations from the anointing that was on these people.

But this is not the first time dead people have ministered the anointing. An impartation of the anointing came to someone who fell on Elisha's grave even after he was dead.

The Principles of Impartation

1. The mystery of impartation occurs when you see the anointed.

"I long to see you" are the words of Apostle Paul. Why did he long to see the people? He wanted to impart to them some spiritual gift. Anytime you are in the presence of an anointed person, expect to experience the anointing. What you see greatly affects you. You remember what you see even more than what you hear. Throughout the Bible, people are encouraged to be vigilant and to remain awake. Why is that? Having eyes wide open, being alert is essential to receiving the anointing.

Jesus said, "The light of the body is the eye: if therefore thine eye be single, the whole body shall be full of light. But if thine eye be evil, thy whole body shall be full of darkness. If therefore the light that is in thee be darkness, how great is that darkness!" (Matthew 6:22,23). This Scripture shows us that your eye is a channel through which light or darkness will enter into your body. The power of God that will enter you through your eye is a light. If your eye is looking for a fault, it will see mistakes and shortcomings and you will be filled with evil spirits. If your eye is full of admiration, you will receive the power and the anointing of God.

The Bible says, "And it came to pass, when they were gone over, that Elijah said unto Elisha, Ask what I shall do for thee, before I be taken away from thee. And Elisha said, I pray thee, let a double portion of thy spirit be upon me. And he said, Thou hast asked a hard thing: nevertheless, if thou see me when I am taken from thee, it shall be so unto thee; but if not, it shall not be so." (2 Kings 2:9,10)

There are things you can get by listening to the anointed but there are things you can only get by watching him in action. When you are in the presence of the anointed, keep your eyes open. An anointed person with his anointing operates in two dimensions of his gifts.

The first dimension is the operation of the things the person teaches or preaches about. This dimension of the anointing is received by listening to the voice of the anointed. The second dimension can be received by watching the anointed. There are many things that are not taught by anointed people. Anointed people just do certain things which they feel they should do. These things are done because they are influenced by the Holy Spirit. They do not even know what they are doing.

Watch with heightened alertness as soon as you see the anointed operating in his anointing. See the characteristics that make the anointed person anointed. For instance, what are the elements that reveal the anointing in the anointed? What are the unusual or supernatural elements that are operating in this anointed person's anointing? I laugh at you if you think that the only supernatural element of an anointed person are when people fall down or when people scream in a service. Perhaps that is the smallest part of the manifestation of the anointing on the anointed.

Watch what the anointed person does not teach about. Watch what he does not talk about. Watch what he does not explain. Watch how he overcomes problems. Watch how he struggles to rise above his limitations. Watch how he overcomes his crises. Some things are absent from every anointed person's teaching. Some things seem so basic to an anointed person that he does not talk about them. Watch out for natural keys of wisdom that the anointed is applying but does not teach. There are certain things that the anointed person experiences but does not teach about. This is why you must see the anointed as well as hear him.

2. The mystery of impartation occurs when you hear the anointed.

The second thing that happens when you see the anointed is that you hear him speaking. When the anointed is speaking, whether in casual conversation, in preaching, in teaching, or even shouting, you must be open to receive the impartation. The Scripture is so clear on this. The spirit entered into Ezekiel "when he spake" to him.

And the spirit entered into me when he spake unto me, and set me upon my feet, that I heard him that spake unto me.

Ezekiel 2:2

The household of Cornelius received the anointing whilst Peter was speaking to the gathering. "While Peter yet spake these words, the Holy Ghost fell on all them which heard the word" (Acts 10:44). Many people have testified of impartation that they received while they were listening to the anointed. I remember a day that I was listening to Benny Hinn speaking and teaching. I suddenly came alive and began to understand many things that he was saying. I had heard him preach many times before on the same subject but I had never received the impartation of such great understanding. The Holy Spirit is also the Spirit of understanding. And when you receive the Spirit of understanding you are receiving an impartation.

There are many ways to detect that the Spirit has been imparted into somebody. What you must look out for is a manifestation of the Spirit. Since the Spirit of understanding (Isaiah 11:2) is part of the Holy Spirit, a sudden great illumination of understanding, knowledge or revelation should alert you to the occurrence of an impartation. The Holy Spirit is not limited to blessing you on fixed Sundays and Wednesdays. Once your heart is opened to the anointed, you must expect an impartation on any day and at any time.

3. The mystery of impartation occurs when you touch the anointed.

Physical contact will always be a point of transmission of something. That is why you should not want to shake hands or hug everybody.

Lay hands suddenly on no man, neither be partaker of other men's sins: keep thyself pure.

1 Timothy 5:22

Unfortunately unbelievers seem to understand this more than Christians. The touch of the anointed with his anointing is important.

Touching will always be important in Christianity. It will never lose its importance. Touching a person with faith becomes more than a greeting, more than an ordinary hug and more than a handshake. The woman with the issue of blood is famous for having faith and touching the hem of Jesus' garment. Through her faith in this great mystery of impartation, she received a powerful healing and was memorialised in Scripture.

And a certain woman, which had an issue of blood twelve years,

And had suffered many things of many physicians, and had spent all that she had, and was nothing bettered, but rather grew worse,

When she had heard of Jesus, came in the press behind, and touched his garment.

For she said, If I may touch but his clothes, I shall be whole.

And straightway the fountain of her blood was dried up; and she felt in her body that she was healed of that plague.

And Jesus, immediately knowing in himself that virtue had gone out of him, turned him about in the press, and said, Who touched my clothes?

And his disciples said unto him, Thou seest the multitude thronging thee, and sayest thou, Who touched me?

And he looked round about to see her that had done this thing.

But the woman fearing and trembling, knowing what was done in her, came and fell down before him, and told him all the truth.

And he said unto her, Daughter, thy faith hath made thee whole; go in peace, and be whole of thy plague.

Mark 5:25-34

The touch is a foundation of our Christian faith. It is called the doctrine of laying on of hands. No matter how high we go in God, we cannot leave the foundations of Christianity. Christianity depends on having great faith in the doctrine of repentance, faith, baptism, resurrection, eternal judgment and laying on of hands.

Therefore leaving the principles of the doctrine of Christ, let us go on unto perfection; not laying again the foundation of repentance from dead works, and of faith toward God,

Of the doctrine of baptisms, and of laying on of hands, and of resurrection of the dead, and of eternal judgment.

Hebrews 6:1-2

4. **The mystery of impartation occurs between people of mutual faith.**

For I long to see you, ... that I may be comforted together with you by the MUTUAL FAITH both of you and me.

Romans 1:11-12

Both the anointed and the one receiving the anointing need to have faith. The anointed must feel the love of God in the people he is ministering to. He must be filled with faith and longing towards the one he is ministering to. Paul was filled with a longing for the Romans. That longing and desire for the Romans was placed there by God. You cannot minister to those who criticize you and hate you. You turn away in your heart from those who despise you and attack you. You do not need to have been to secondary school to know this.

The receivers of the anointing must equally desire the gift. The one condition for receiving the gift of the spirit is desire. That is why Paul said to the Corinthians, "...desire spiritual gifts, but rather that ye may prophesy" (1 Corinthians 14:1). Those who are receiving the anointing must be open and admiring of the anointed and his anointing. They must be filled with desire if the gift of the spirit is to fall on them.

5. **The mystery of impartation results in your establishment.**

For I long to see you, that I may impart unto you some spiritual gift, to the end ye may be ESTABLISHED;

Romans 1:11

The impartation of the anointing leads to your establishment. You become established in your ministry when you have received the gift. Andrae Crouch became established in the music world because of the gift that he had. Your establishment depends on the mystery of impartation. Do not downplay this reality. You will need a gift if you are ever to become established in anything you do.

6. The mystery of impartation results in your comfort.

For I long to see you, that I may impart unto you some spiritual gift, to the end ye may be established; That is, that I may be COMFORTED together with you ...

Romans 1:11-12

The mystery of impartation results in your comfort, your encouragement and your consolation. There is a lot of sadness in this world. There is a lot of sorrow and depression. There is a lot of hopelessness. Without the gift of God you will walk around in hopelessness and great discouragement in your life. The mystery of impartation will provide a supernatural gift that will change the landscape of your life and comfort you greatly.

7. The mystery of impartation benefits the anointed because he receives eternal fruit from whoever is blessed through his anointing.

For I long to see you ... that I might HAVE SOME FRUIT among you also, even as among other Gentiles

Romans 1:11, 13

Perhaps, the greatest blessing of the mystery of impartation is the release of eternal fruit into your life. Anybody who has received an impartation through your life and ministry becomes a part of you. You share in the person's fruit and you have shares in what he accomplishes for eternity. It is in your interest to share the grace of God and the gift He has given you with as many people as possible so that you can have fruit for eternity.

CHAPTER 12

Do Not Miss Subtle and Casual Anointings

And as they departed, Jesus began to say unto the multitudes concerning John, What went ye out into the wilderness to see? A reed shaken with the wind? But what went ye out for to see? A man clothed in soft raiment? Behold, they that wear soft clothing are in kings 'houses. But what went ye out for to see? A prophet? Yea, I say unto you, and more than a prophet.

For this is he, of whom it is written, Behold, I send my messenger before thy face, which shall prepare thy way before thee. Verily I say unto you, among them that are born of women there hath not risen a greater than John the Baptist: notwithstanding he that is least in the kingdom of heaven is greater than he.

Matthew 11:7-11

It is important to recognize subtle and casually expressed anointings. Many things are supernatural but may not be spectacular. Many things are powerful but may not strike you as magical. Many times, outsiders recognize the anointing faster when it is casual or subtle.

I remember a time I chatted with a prominent businessman from my city. I was sitting on my easy chair, because I never sit behind a desk. As we chatted he looked at me and said, "You are very deceptive about who you are."

'Why?" I asked.

He said, "You look very casual, as if you are relaxing here doing nothing much. But that is not the case at all. You are leading, managing, organising massive operations involving many people at the same time. But there is no sign on you about the level of stress and the size of operation you are involved in."

Laban was the first person to recognize the power that was working on Israel. He was an outsider but he recognized that there was something unusual at work. Today the power of God still rests on Israel. It has become a mighty nation against all odds. It has withstood the persecution through the centuries. It is a blessed nation with more inventors, Nobel Prize winners and intelligent people than most nations. Israel has become the richest community within America with more billionaires and rich people than any other group of people. Yet, it was Laban who recognized that the power of God was resting on this young man who was to produce this nation.

It would be quite easy to miss the power of God on Jesus Christ. Jesus was someone who went around eating with sinners. Jesus was someone who was despised by the religious authorities of the day. Jesus' followers were fishermen. Few rich men, if any, joined the fold. Large numbers of women followed Jesus, ministering to Him. All these and many more would lead to great questions about the greatness of Jesus Christ. If you do not have eyes of the anointing you could easily join those who crucified him. Yet, Nicodemus had eyes to see the power of God at work in the Son of God. Often it is outsiders who recognize the anointed when he is operating in a subtle or casual anointing. Nicodemus told Jesus, "No one could do this unless God was with him".

Elisha was a truly casual prophet. He did not desire greatness and was not even interested in gaining favours with commanders of foreign armies. It was a little maid who pointed out to the great commander, Naaman that there was a casual prophet called Elisha who could heal him of his disease.

But Elisha did not bother to show Naaman certain courtesies. Elisha did not even come out of his house to greet Naaman. Elisha did not have any dramatic expression of the anointing. He stayed indoors and sent a message to Naaman. "Go and have a bath in a river Jordan." How unimpressive can a prophet be? How could he minister healing by sending such a bland message through a messenger?

Today, many people miss the anointing for the same reason that Naaman almost did. How unexciting Elisha must have been to onlookers. And yet there was great power being manifested through the ministry of Elisha. Do not miss the power of God because of its bland and non-spectacular nature.

1. **Nicodemus recognized the subtle anointing of Jesus Christ.**

    There was a man of the Pharisees, named Nicodemus, a ruler of the Jews: The same came to Jesus by night, and said unto him, Rabbi, we know that thou art a teacher come from God: for no man can do these miracles that thou doest, except God be with him.

    John 3:1-2

2. **Laban first recognized the anointing on Israel.**

    And Laban said unto him, I pray thee, if I have found favour in thine eyes, tarry: for I have learned by experience that the Lord hath blessed me for thy sake.

    Genesis 30:27

3. A little maid recognized the anointing on casual Elisha.

Now Naaman, captain of the host of the king of Syria, was a great man with his master, and honourable, because by him the LORD had given deliverance unto Syria: he was also a mighty man in valour, but he was a leper. And the Syrians had gone out by companies, and had brought away captive out of the land of Israel a little maid; and she waited on Naaman's wife.

And she said unto her mistress, Would God my lord were with the prophet that is in Samaria! for he would recover him of his leprosy. And one went in, and told his lord, saying, Thus and thus said the maid that is of the land of Israel.

2 Kings 5:1-4

CHAPTER 13

The Honour and the Anointing

But Jesus said unto them, A PROPHET IS NOT WITHOUT HONOUR, but in his own country, and among his own kin, and in his own house.

And HE COULD THERE DO NO MIGHTY WORK, save that he laid his hands upon a few sick folk, and healed them.

Mark 6:4-5

1. Where the anointing is not honoured it does not work.

And he went out from thence, and came into his own country; and his disciples follow him. And when the sabbath day was come, he began to teach in the synagogue: and many hearing him were astonished, saying, From whence hath this man these things? And what wisdom is this which is given unto him, that even such mighty works are wrought by his hands? Is not this the carpenter, the son of Mary, the brother of James, and Joses, and of Juda, and Simon? And are not his sisters here with us? And they were offended at him.

But Jesus said unto them, A PROPHET IS NOT WITHOUT HONOUR, but in his own country, and among his own kin, and in his own house.

And HE COULD THERE DO NO MIGHTY WORK, save that he laid his hands upon a few sick folk, and healed them.

Mark 6:1-5

Where the anointing is not honoured, it does not work. Many men of God walk around, having great gifts to impart. Unfortunately, the anointing on their lives is not imparted to anyone and the power of God seems to not to work the way it should. This is nothing strange. It happened in the life and ministry of Jesus. When He went to His hometown He was not honoured. Instead, He was despised, ridiculed, questioned, interrogated! He was accused. He was challenged. His background was investigated. His family history was dug up and His message was not even listened to.

Jesus was heavily anointed. He was so anointed that He could raise the dead, cleanse lepers, walk on water, rebuke storms and speak great prophecies. But the anointing simply did not work in Nazareth where He was not honoured.

There is no anointed person who can function properly where he is not honoured. There is no group of people who will truly benefit from the anointed servant of God if they do not honour him. This is why some pastors seem to have a greater impact outside their own churches than within their own churches. This is because they are honoured, respected and received as very great people outside their home church circles.

I know a famous healing evangelist who is greatly admired outside his own country. He is a hero to many. Entire cities will gather to hear him. But in his own country, where he is not honoured, he will struggle to have two thousand people listening to him. This is also why the devil tries so hard to discredit servants of God. Satan is trying to take away their honour. He knows that the anointing of the man of God will not work where he is not honoured.

2. Honouring the anointing is an obligation and a legal requirement.

Let him that is taught in the word communicate unto him that teacheth in all good things. Be not deceived; God is not mocked: for whatsoever a man soweth, that shall he also reap.

Galatians 6:6-7

Honouring the anointed is an obligation for those who have been blessed, healed and delivered by the anointing. Galatians 6:6 is clear on this divine obligation. Galatians 6:6 teaches that Christians should take their carnal, natural possessions and honour the anointed by giving to him.

Amazingly, Galatians 6:7 follows Galatians 6:6. Galatians 6:7 is the famous verse that is used to declare curses and blessings on people. You must have heard it said, "You will reap what you have sown." What most people do not realise is that Galatians 6:7 is a continuation of Galatians 6:6. The greatest promise for sowing and reaping has to do with honouring the anointed who has taught you and fed you with the Word of God.

In every church, there are two possible trends: increasing honour and decreasing honour.

Decreasing Honour in a Church

The decreasing honour is a natural progression you can expect in a church. A pastor is less and less appreciated as the years go by. His gifts, his talents and his great leadership are taken for granted as the years go by. Everyone expects good things, proper things and nice things, as that has been the standard they have experienced for many years. Also, as the years go by, the natural weaknesses, deficiencies, personality traits and temperament of the anointed become more pronounced or more obvious to the congregation. This can lead them to think that there is not much to their anointed pastor because he has the traits of an ordinary human being. When Jesus walked amongst us, He dined among His disciples and slept among them on many occasions. He must have also used the toilet on many occasions. Over time, Jesus' natural traits must have been obvious. This leads to a decline in the honour, respect and appreciation that a servant of God receives.

Increasing Honour in a Church

A trend of increasing honour in a church can only come about by teaching the subject, emphasizing the Word of God and leading the congregation to appreciate the gift of God in their midst. Most people simply do what they are taught. Without teaching, the congregation will not improve their appreciation. I know churches where the impact of the pastor is great within the church because there is a strong maintenance of the appreciation culture in that congregation. The pastor himself may strongly introduce himself and inform the congregation of their need to appreciate and recognize the gift that God has placed in their midst. This is important so that the congregation does not miss the blessings of the anointing. What is the point of having such a great gift in your midst and not benefitting from it? What is the point of having the biggest river in your city and yet have a shortage of water? What is the use of bread you cannot eat and money that you cannot use? What is the use of an employee who is not allowed to work for you?

Decide to increasingly honour the anointed in your midst to provoke a great blessing for your life and ministry.

3. Your honouring the anointing must be done according to the rank at which you receive.

He that receiveth a prophet in the name of a prophet shall receive a prophet's reward; and he that receiveth a righteous man in the name of a righteous man shall receive a righteous man's reward.

Matthew 10:41

God's servant must be honoured according to your faith. Every human being can be treated in different ways. A man can be treated as a father, a brother, a friend, a junior pastor, an associate pastor, a great pastor, a prophet, an apostle, a businessman, a pianist or even a fool. In my experience, I have been treated in so many different ways. It simply depends on how the person sees you. The reward or blessing you receive from a person is according to the rank or name in which you receive the person. If you receive the person as a pianist you receive a pianist's reward. If you receive a person as an associate pastor you receive the blessing of an associate pastor. If you treat the person as a great apostle, you receive the blessing of a great apostle. If you receive the person as a teacher, you will receive the blessing of a teacher.

Some people receive me as a pastor and they receive the blessings of a pastor through me. There are others who receive me as a prophet and they receive the blessings of a prophet through me. I know churches that receive me as a great apostle. There, they receive the blessings that a great apostle can deliver.

It is easy to see the confusion in Christians when they try to appreciate God's servants. Sometimes, they do exactly the same thing for the apostle, prophet or founder of the church, as they would do for the associate or junior pastor. I once visited a church that was presenting two gifts to two different pastors. They presented exactly the same birthday card with the same offering to the senior pastor who had founded the church as they did to a much junior assistant pastor who had been ordained by the senior pastor. Obviously, they had not realised that they were receiving both of them as men of the same rank.

I remember a church in which a visiting minister was presented with a brand new Toyota Land Cruiser as a gift from an appreciative congregant who had been in the service when this visiting minister preached. Unfortunately, this appreciative congregant had never honoured the founder and senior pastor who had been preaching to him for more than twenty years with even a bicycle. The one who preaches to you everyday, brings you up in the Lord and covers you for twenty years must be in a far higher rank as far as you are concerned when compared to a visitor whom you have encountered for three days. You would not even know about the visiting minister if your own pastor had not welcomed him into the church.

4. Honouring the anointing provokes unspeakable blessings on your behalf.

And it fell on a day, that Elisha passed to Shunem, where was a great woman; and SHE CONSTRAINED HIM TO EAT BREAD. And so it was, that as oft as he passed by, he turned in thither to eat bread. And she said unto her husband, Behold now, I perceive that this is an holy man of God, which passeth by us continually.

LET US MAKE A LITTLE CHAMBER, I pray thee, on the wall; and LET US SET FOR HIM THERE A BED, AND A TABLE, AND A STOOL, AND A CANDLESTICK: and it shall be, when he cometh to us, that he shall turn in thither

And it fell on a day, that he came thither, and he turned into the chamber, and lay there. And he said to Gehazi his servant, Call this Shunammite. And when he had called her, she stood before him. And he said unto him, Say now unto her, Behold, thou hast been careful for us with all this care; what is to be done for thee? wouldest thou be spoken for to the king, or to the captain of the host?

And she answered, I dwell among mine own people. And he said, What then is to be done for her? And Gehazi answered, Verily she hath no child, and her husband is old. And he said, Call her. And when he had called her, she stood in the door. And he said, About this season, according to the time of life, thou shalt embrace a son. And she said, Nay, my lord, thou man of God, do not lie unto thine handmaid. And the woman conceived, and bare a son at that season that Elisha had said unto her, according to the time of life.

2 Kings 4:8-17

There are some important points to glean from the story of Elisha and the Shunamite woman.

1. She took a quality decision to honour the anointed.

2. She began to honour the anointed at a lower level. This lower level was the honour she bestowed on him by giving him bread and food.

3. The Shunamite woman moved to a much higher level of honouring the anointed. She did this by building a house for him and by furnishing it. She honoured him at this highest level by making his life comfortable.

4. The power of God on Elisha was provoked after he had received the honour from this woman.

   Elisha did not ask about the woman's needs when he was eating her bread. He only asked about her needs when she built the room and he stayed in the room enjoying the candle, the table and the chair that she had made for him.

5. The Shunamite woman received the great blessing of pregnancy, even though her husband was an old man. The stark reality of the old age of her husband is mentioned as a great natural obstacle to this woman receiving a miracle child. There was no river too wide, no mountain high and no distance too high for God's power after the anointing had been honoured.

5. Honour the anointing in a substantial way.

But thou hast not called upon me, O Jacob; but thou hast been weary of me, O Israel. Thou hast not brought me the small cattle of thy burnt offerings; NEITHER HAST THOU HONOURED ME WITH THY SACRIFICES. I have not caused thee to serve with an offering, nor wearied thee with incense.

Thou hast bought me no sweet cane with money, NEITHER HAST THOU FILLED ME WITH THE FAT OF THY SACRIFICES: but thou hast made me to serve with thy sins, thou hast wearied me with thine iniquities

Isaiah 43:22-24

The great prophet Isaiah speaks forth the word of the Lord concerning the honour of the anointed. He gives details about the honour that he is expecting. This great passage reveals that God expects to be honoured substantially.

God expects you to honour the anointed with your riches and with the best that you have. God asks several questions:

1. Why have you not brought me some of your small cattle?

2. Why have you not honoured me with sacrifices?

3. Why have you not brought me some sweet cane?

4. Why have you not brought me money?

5. Why have you not brought me the fat of the sacrifice?

6. Why have I only been burdened with your sins and your problems?

You see, it is important to honour the anointing substantially. It is important to honour the anointed with your riches. God is expecting the honour to come through your money, your cattle, your sweet cane and the fat of your sacrifices. Are you doing that today? Or are you honouring the servant of the Lord with worthless gifts and sacrifices?

6. **Do not honour the anointed with inappropriate and worthless things.**

    And if ye offer the blind for sacrifice, is it not evil? And if ye offer the lame and sick, is it not evil? Offer it now unto thy governor; will he be pleased with thee, or accept thy person? Saith the Lord of hosts.

    Malachi 1:8

    In the days of Malachi, just as it happens today, people bring worthless things to the house of God and to the servant of God. Everyone has a box of perfume that he has not yet used. Everyone has a vase or chinaware that she cannot use. Everyone has some clothes that do not fit very well. These are the things that are brought to honour the anointing. You are making a great mistake. God is not a fool. When you honour the anointed, it is God you are honouring and not a man.

    An anointed man is nothing. He has nothing to give you. Neither does he have any blessing to bestow upon you. It is God alone who blesses. If you despise God and treat Him like a fool, you will receive an appropriate harvest. Do not think you are dealing with a man. Think of the reality that you are dealing with God.

7. **They that honour the anointing will be honoured.**

    Wherefore the Lord God of Israel saith, I said indeed that thy house, and the house of thy father, should walk before me for ever: but now the Lord saith, Be it far from me; for THEM THAT HONOUR ME I WILL HONOUR, AND THEY THAT DESPISE ME SHALL BE LIGHTLY ESTEEMED.

    1 Samuel 2:30

    Eli the prophet honoured his sons above the Lord. "Wherefore kick ye at my sacrifice and at mine offering, which I have commanded in my habitation; and honourest thy sons above me, to make yourselves fat with the chiefest of all the offerings of Israel my people?" (1 Samuel 2:29). You must watch out for what you honour above God. Most of us have something that we honour above the Lord. Some of us honour presidents. Some of us honour politicians. Some of us honour the rich above the honour that we give to the Lord.

Perhaps you give to the governor, the president or the politician far more than you do to the pastor. To the politician, you give thousands of dollars but for the pastor, you buy a ten-dollar toy car and a ten-dollar doll for his children. You go to his house and present a large box of these toys that you know are valueless. The real substantial donations you make are never to God or His servants. Do not forget what God says in His words. "He that honours me, I will honour. He that despises me I will lightly esteem." Today, you may be lightly esteemed because you have not honoured the Lord, you have not honoured His anointed and His anointing. It is time to sow seeds of honour so that you can experience the honour that only God can give you.

8. Honouring the anointed will result in your establishment.

Lord, who shall abide in thy tabernacle? Who shall dwell in thy holy hill?

He that walketh uprightly, and worketh righteousness, and speaketh the truth in his heart. He that backbiteth not with his tongue, nor doeth evil to his neighbour, nor taketh up a reproach against his neighbour.

In whose eyes a vile person is contemned; but he honoureth them that fear the Lord. He that sweareth to his own hurt, and changeth not

Psalm 15:1-4

Who is going to experience the power of God and dwell in the holy hill of God? Someone who despises and rejects evil men. Not only does he despise and reject evil men, but he honours people who fear God. You see, it is not enough to despise and reject evil. You must rise up and honour people who fear God.

It is the servants of the Lord who fear God. It is the anointed men who are servants of the Lord and who fear the Lord. You must decide to become one of the people who fear the Lord.

I have attended a number of different funerals. At funerals you have an idea of how a person lived. What a joy it is to attend the funeral of someone who lived in and around the church; who feared God and who served God with his life. The choirs of the church, the groups in the church and even the pastors acknowledge that this dead person once lived his life in the fear of God. He certainly would not have been perfect but he lived in the fear of God. Honouring God is an important thing because it provokes the blessing of the Lord.

Honouring of the anointing in the ministry of Jesus

All these twenty two miracles show a great honouring of the anointing.

1. The healing of blind Bartimaeus (Mark 10:46-52).

2. The healing of the blind man by the pool of Siloam (John 9:1-17).

3. The healing of the blind man who saw men as trees (Mark 8:22-26).

4. The healing of the two blind men who followed Jesus to Jairus' house (Matthew 9:27-31).

5. The healing of the woman with the issue of blood (Mark 5:25-34).

6. The healing of the mad man of Gadara (Mark 5:1-16).

7. The healing of the paralytic who was led down the roof (Mark 2:1-5).

8. The healing of the man with the withered hand (Matthew 12:9-13).

9. The healing of the dumb man (Matthew 9:32-33).

10. The healing of the deaf and dumb man (Mark 7:31-37).

11. The healing of the woman who had been bent over for eighteen years (Luke 13:11-17).

12. The healing of the man who had been ill for thirty-eight years (John 5:2-9).

13. The healing of the epileptic boy (Matthew 17:14-18).

14. The healing of the ten lepers (Luke 17:12-19).

15. The healing of the leper (Matthew 8:1-4).

16. The healing of the Syro-Phoenician woman's daughter (Matthew 15:21-28).

17. The healing of the nobleman's son (John 4:46-54).

18. The healing of the centurion's servant (Luke 7:1-10).

19. The healing of Peter's mother-in-law (Luke 4:38-39).

20. The widow of Nain's son raised from the dead (Luke 7:11-15).

21. Jairus' daughter raised from the dead (Mark 5:22-24, 35-42).

22. Raising Lazarus from the dead (John 11:1-47).

CHAPTER 14

How Jesus Celebrated the Woman Who Honoured the Anointing

And being in Bethany in the house of Simon the leper, as he sat at meat, there came a woman having an alabaster box of ointment of spikenard very precious; and she brake the box, and poured it on his head.

And there were some that had indignation within themselves, and said, Why was this waste of the ointment made? For it might have been sold for more than three hundred pence, and have been given to the poor. And they murmured against her.

And Jesus said, Let her alone; why trouble ye her? she hath wrought a good work on me.

For ye have the poor with you always, and whensoever ye will ye may do them good:but me ye have not always. She hath done what she could: she is come aforehand to anoint my body to the burying.

Mark 14:3-8

This story has several noteworthy points:

1. **A great expense was bestowed on Jesus Christ.** And yet, Jesus received and accepted this great and expensive thing that was done. Jesus did not rebuke the woman or curse her. Jesus did not say that she had done something that was wrong.

2. **Some people considered the great expense to be a great waste.** But Jesus did not think so. Jesus thought it was a good thing that the woman had done. In fact Jesus asked people to leave her alone and not to bother or trouble her for what she had done.

3. **Jesus accepted the honour that was done Him and made many eternal comments about her.** Today there are several pastors who reject the honour and riches bestowed on them because of the anointing. What you must realise is that people are honouring the great power of God that flows through you.

4. **Jesus said, "She has wrought a good work."** Jesus said this woman was doing the right thing. Jesus said this woman had done a good thing and a good work had been accomplished. If Jesus thinks it is a good thing then it must be a good thing.

5. **Jesus said, "She has done what she could."** I once visited a retreat centre which had the names of different people who had contributed to that retreat centre. On one of the doors I saw the name of a woman who had contributed to the building of that room with the inscription "She has done what she could". I was touched by this statement - "She has done what she could!" There are people who cannot do much. But they do what they can. Perhaps you do not have the anointing or the gifts to minister to thousands. Perhaps you do not have the gift of healing. Perhaps your life is so messed up that you may never qualify for a pulpit ministry. Perhaps all you can do is to honour the anointed. Please do it. You will be memorialised for honouring the anointed!

6. **Jesus Christ prophesied that this woman would always be remembered.** Jesus memorialised the woman who honoured the anointing on His life. He said that she would be remembered everywhere the gospel was preached. Today as I write this book the words of Jesus are being fulfilled. She is being remembered, she is being written about, she is being used as a good example.

7. **Jesus commented on the wisdom and the foresight of this woman.** Jesus commented that this woman, moving by the Spirit, had actually anointed Him for His burial. In other words He was not going to miss His burial anointing because of this woman. Jesus would not have been anointed at His burial because he was to rise from the dead too quickly for that ceremony to take place. No one was going to have the honour of anointing Him.

In conclusion, honouring the anointing is a good work. It is something that is recommended by Jesus. It is not at all a sign of luxury, opulence or extravagance. Our Saviour does not reject the honouring of the anointing with expensive things. Indeed, she is the only person in the Bible of whom it is prophesied that wherever the gospel is preached she will be remembered. Is it not a fulfilment of the Scripture, "He who honours me I will honour and he who despises me I will despise"?

CHAPTER 15

Where the Anointing is Honoured it Works Wonders

And BY A PROPHET the Lord brought Israel out of Egypt, and BY A PROPHET was he preserved.

Hosea 12:13

Where the anointing is honoured, the anointed man becomes an agent for many great blessings for God's people. "By a prophet" means through the agency of a prophet! Through God's prophet acting as an agent, you will experience many great and unbelievable things. Most people see their jobs as the agents of their blessing. Some people see their parents as the agent of their blessing. Others see their marriage as the agent of their blessing. This Scripture shows us that the prophet was the agent through which Israel was delivered from Egypt. This great Scripture also shows us that a prophet was the agent through which Israel was protected and preserved. Through many dangers, toils and snares, Israel was preserved and kept by the agency of a prophet.

Anointed people are strange people who are used by God to accomplish wonderful things. It is important to recognize the anointed person amongst you. Through anointed people God has brought deliverance, healing, promotion and advancement to many lives. The human race is plagued with evil spirits that suck away the lives of the carriers thereof.

All through the Bible, you can learn how God uses anointed people as agents of change and deliverance. It is your turn to be advanced in this life through one of God's agents of change and blessing. These agents of blessing and change are those we call "anointed". They are anointed because God has filled them with His power and His Spirit. It is not everyone who has the Holy Spirit on him or in him. Some people are specially given the Holy Spirit in a large measure. Usually, the larger the measure of the Holy Spirit on a person, the more power and gifts he displays in his ministry.

In the next few paragraphs, I want you to see the kind of blessing and change that come through these powerful and anointed agents of God. You will discover that an anointed person is an agent of many good things that God has for His children.

Elisha was probably the most anointed person in the Old Testament because he carried a double portion of the anointing of Elijah. It is important to see Elisha more as an anointed person than even a prophet.

1. The anointed is an agent of deliverance from armed men.

Then the king sent unto him a captain of fifty with his fifty. And he went up to him: and, behold, he sat on the top of an hill. And he spake unto him, Thou man of God, the king hath said, Come down.

And Elijah answered and said to the captain of fifty, if I be a man of God, then let fire come down from heaven, and consume thee and thy fifty. And there came down fire from heaven, and consumed him and his fifty.

2 Kings 1:9-10

Elijah, the anointed person, was the agent of deliverance from an army of armed men. The prophet was about to be killed by a captain of fifty with his fifty. Through the words of the anointed person, fifty armed men with their captain were removed from this earth. You will be set free from those who think they can destroy you by force. Today is the last day that anyone will ever think of attacking you with physical force. I curse the activities of armed robbers in your life from today!

2. The anointed is an agent of the anointing.

And it came to pass, when they were gone over, that Elijah said unto Elisha, Ask what I shall do for thee, before I be taken away from thee. And Elisha said, I pray thee, let a double portion of thy spirit be upon me.

And he said, Thou hast asked a hard thing: nevertheless, if thou see me when I am taken from thee, it shall be so unto thee; but if not, it shall not be so.

2 Kings 2:9-10

Anointed people are agents for you to receive the anointing. Through an anointed person, you can receive the power of God and the gift that will promote you and lift you up to the place you are called to be. The power you lack is found in the anointing. The anointing is found in the anointed. As you get closer to the anointed, you will receive the anointing.

Elisha received the anointing through Elijah. He asked Elijah for the anointing because he realised that Elijah was an agent through whom he could receive the anointing. Elijah's answer was simple, "I know I am an agent of the anointing. You have asked a hard thing but if you see me going you will receive the anointing". Indeed, Elisha witnessed the departure of Elijah and received the mantle of his father Elijah. Elisha would never have received twice as much of the anointing if he had not met with Elijah. It was through Elijah's words that Elisha became anointed.

3. The anointed is an agent of improvement.

And the men of the city said unto Elisha, Behold, I pray thee, the situation of this city is pleasant, as my lord seeth: but the water is naught, and the ground barren.

And he said, Bring me a new cruse, and put salt therein. And they brought it to him.

And he went forth unto the spring of the waters, and cast the salt in there, and said, Thus saith the LORD, I have healed these waters; there shall not be from thence any more death or barren land.

So the waters were healed unto this day, according to the saying of Elisha which he spake.

2 Kings 2:19-22

Through the anointing on Elisha, the city received good drinking water. The men of the city informed Elisha that the city was pleasant and nice to stay in, but they simply did not have good drinking water. Elisha performed a miracle by putting salt into the water and it was immediately purified. From that time onwards, the city had good drinking water.

4. The anointed is an agent of the will of God.

God had decided to end the life of King Ahaziah. King Ahaziah was a rebellious man who was consulting Baalzebub, the god of Ekron about whether he would recover from his illness. These messengers encountered Elijah on the way to consult this idol.

...Is it because there is no god in Israel that you are going to inquire of Baalzebub the god of Ekron? Now therefore, thus says the LORD, You shall not come down from the bed where you have gone up but you shall surely die.

2 Kings 1:3

The will of God and the judgment of God was that King Ahaziah should die. Elijah, the anointed one, delivered the will and the mind of God plainly and fearlessly to the king. There was no playing about. There was no politics and there was no bottom licking as you find in men of God today.

A truly anointed person is an agent of the will of God. And sometimes the will of God is judgment.

5. The anointed is an agent of victory for every battle in your life.

And Elisha said unto the king of Israel, What have I to do with thee? get thee to the prophets of thy father, and to the prophets of thy mother. And the king of Israel said unto him, Nay: for the Lord hath called these three kings together, to deliver them into the hand of Moab.

And Elisha said, As the Lord of hosts liveth, before whom I stand, surely, were it not that I regard the presence of Jehoshaphat the king of Judah, I would not look toward thee, nor see thee.

But now bring me a minstrel. And it came to pass, when the minstrel played, that the hand of the Lord came upon him. And he said, Thus saith the Lord, Make this valley full of ditches. For thus saith the Lord, Ye shall not see wind, neither shall ye see rain; yet that valley shall be filled with water, that ye may drink, both ye, and your cattle, and your beasts.

And this is but a light thing in the sight of the Lord: he will deliver the Moabites also into your hand. And ye shall smite every fenced city, and every choice city, and shall fell every good tree, and stop all wells of water, and mar every good piece of land with stones.

2 Kings 3:13-19

Jehoshaphat, the king of Judah, wrought a great victory over the king of Moab through the anointed words of Elijah the prophet. Jehoshaphat, the king of Judah and Jehoram, the king of Israel were terrified by the king of Moab. "Then the king of Israel said, Alas! For the Lord has called these three kings to give them into the hand of Moab. But Jehoshaphat said, Is there not a prophet of the Lord here that we may inquire of the LORD by him?" (2 Kings 3:10-11).

In other words, is there not an anointed person through whom we may achieve the victory in this battle and gain the upper hand in this situation? Indeed, there was! One of the king's servants reminded them that Elisha, the son of Shaphat was in town. Elisha was carrying a double portion of the anointing that Elijah had. It was not just because Elisha was a prophet. It was because of the anointing on his life. It is the anointing that makes someone into a prophet. The anointing is the key element that is working. It is the anointing that enables the anointed person to be an agent for your victory.

6. The anointed is an agent for your prosperity.

Now there cried a certain woman of the wives of the sons of the prophets unto Elisha, saying, Thy servant my husband is dead; and thou knowest that thy servant did fear the LORD: and the creditor is come to take unto him my two sons to be bondmen.

And Elisha said unto her, What shall I do for thee? tell me, what hast thou in the house? And she said, Thine handmaid hath not any thing in the house, save a pot of oil.

Then he said, Go, borrow thee vessels abroad of all thy neighbours, even empty vessels; borrow not a few.

And when thou art come in, thou shalt shut the door upon thee and upon thy sons, and shalt pour out into all those vessels, and thou shalt set aside that which is full.

So she went from him, and shut the door upon her and upon her sons, who brought the vessels to her; and she poured out.

And it came to pass, when the vessels were full, that she said unto her son, Bring me yet a vessel. And he said unto her, There is not a vessel more. And the oil stayed.

Then she came and told the man of God. And he said, Go, sell the oil, and pay thy debt, and live thou and thy children of the rest.

2 Kings 4:1-7

Through the anointed man, a widow suffering from an overwhelming desolation was delivered and released into her prosperity. Your prosperity will come when you start to respect the anointed and his God-given power to be an agent for your prosperity.

Many people do not respect the anointed and his anointing and therefore do not benefit from it. There were many widows in the days of Elijah the prophet, but he was not sent to any of them save the widow of Sarepta. There are always a lot of people in need of prosperity. It is those whose hearts are touched to received from the anointed who benefit from the anointed. You must be very careful when dealing with the anointed. Even your dislike and your hatred for an anointed person is a dangerous feeling to have.

Notice this Scripture: "But I shall crush his adversaries before him and strike those who hate him" (Psalm 89:23). Another version says, "I will beat down his foes before his face and plague them that hate him."

7.   The anointed is an agent for your healing.

And she said unto her husband, Behold now, I perceive that this is an holy man of God, which passeth by us continually.

Let us make a little chamber, I pray thee, on the wall; and let us set for him there a bed, and a table, and a stool, and a candlestick: and it shall be, when he cometh to us, that he shall turn in thither.

And it fell on a day, that he came thither, and he turned into the chamber, and lay there.

And he said to Gehazi his servant, Call this Shunammite. And when he had called her, she stood before him.

And he said unto him, Say now unto her, Behold, thou hast been careful for us with all this care; what is to be done for thee? wouldest thou be spoken for to the king, or to the captain of the host? And she answered, I dwell among mine own people.

And he said, What then is to be done for her? And Gehazi answered, Verily she hath no child, and her husband is old.

And he said, Call her. And when he had called her, she stood in the door.

And he said, About this season, according to the time of life, thou shalt embrace a son. And she said, Nay, my lord, thou man of God, do not lie unto thine handmaid.

And the woman conceived, and bare a son at that season that Elisha had said unto her, according to the time of life.

2 Kings 4:9-17

Through the anointed, you will receive healing from every plague and every kind of disease in this world. The Shunammite woman received a child because she believed in the anointed and honoured him. She showed her respect for the anointed by furnishing a room permanently for the man of God. This provoked the man of God to ask what she needed. Indeed, every rich and apparently successful person has a need. She needed a child and she needed one desperately.

Elisha's words were simple: "At this time next year, you shall embrace a son." It is noteworthy that Gehazi pointed out to Elisha that the woman's husband was old. This old husband would hardly ever have sex with his wife, the Shunammite woman. The old man was probably suffering from low sperm count, impotence and erectile dysfunction. All these problems were overcome through the anointing. Through the anointed and his anointing, all the complicated problems of your life will be dissolved.

8. The anointed is an agent for your greatest miracle.

Then she said, Did I desire a son of my lord? Did I not say, Do not deceive me?

Then he said to Gehazi, Gird up thy loins, and take my staff in thine hand, and go thy way: if thou meet any man, salute him not; and if any salute thee, answer him not again: and lay my staff upon the face of the child.

And the mother of the child said, As the Lord liveth, and as thy soul liveth, I will not leave thee. And he arose, and followed her. And Gehazi passed on before them, and laid the staff upon the face of the child; but there was neither voice, nor hearing. Wherefore he went again to meet him, and told him, saying, the child is not awaked.

And when Elisha was come into the house, behold, the child was dead, and laid upon his bed. He went in therefore, and shut the door upon them twain, and prayed unto the LORD.

And he went up, and lay upon the child, and put his mouth upon his mouth, and his eyes upon his eyes, and his hands upon his hands: and he stretched himself upon the child; and the flesh of the child waxed warm.

Then he returned, and walked in the house to and fro; and went up, and stretched himself upon him: and the child sneezed seven times, and the child opened his eyes.

And he called Gehazi, and said, Call this Shunammite. So he called her. And when she was come in unto him, he said, take up thy son.

Then she went in, and fell at his feet, and bowed herself to the ground, and took up her son, and went out.

2 Kings 4:28-37

The Shunammite woman's son grew up and died suddenly. He woke up one day and exclaimed, "My head, my head!" He was carried to his mother and sat on her lap till midday when he died. This woman was experienced in getting miracles out of the anointed. She knew where to go to solve the unsolvable and break the unbreakable. Instead of sending someone, she went herself on a donkey all the way to Mount Carmel. The prophet Elisha saw her at a distance and sent Gehazi to find out what was happening. When he got to know that the son had died, he knew that his anointing was being called upon again.

Sometimes, one person receives more than one blessing from an anointed person. He that hath shall have more and he that hath not shall lose even that which he has.

9. The anointed is an agent that delivers you from death.

And Elisha came again to Gilgal: and *there was* a dearth in the land; and the sons of the prophets *were* sitting before him: and he said unto his servant, Set on the great pot, and seethe pottage for the sons of the prophets.

And one went out into the field to gather herbs, and found a wild vine, and gathered thereof wild gourds his lap full, and came and shred *them* into the pot of pottage: for they knew *them* not. So they poured out for the men to eat. And it came to pass, as they were eating of the pottage, that they cried out, and said, O *thou* man of God, *there is* death in the pot. And they could not eat *thereof.*

But he said, then bring meal. And he cast *it* into the pot; and he said, Pour out for the people, that they may eat. And there was no harm in the pot.

2 Kings 4:38-41

One day, there was an accident in which some young prophets went into the field to gather herbs to make some stew.

Unfortunately, someone found a wild vine and sliced it into the pot of stew. As they began to eat this food they realised that it was poisoned. Death was about to strike a whole group of prophets who were enjoying a meal. The anointed simply performed a miracle in which he threw in some flour. Then he said, "There is no harm in the pot. You can eat the stew." The poisonous stew of death was turned into a healthy pot of stew. They enjoyed a balanced diet with a lot of vegetables because of the anointed with his anointing.

10. The anointed is an agent for your abundance.

And there came a man from Baalshalisha, and brought the man of God bread of the firstfruits, twenty loaves of barley, and full ears of corn in the husk thereof. And he said, give unto the people, that they may eat.

And his servitor said, What, should I set this before an hundred men? He said again, Give the people, that they may eat: for thus saith the Lord, They shall eat, and shall leave *thereof.*

So he set *it* before them, and they did eat, and left *thereof,* according to the word of the Lord.

2 Kings 4:42-44

There was an occasion where an offering was brought to Elisha. This offering consisted of twenty loaves of bread and some fresh corn. Elisha asked that it be given to the people. Everyone thought the food would not be enough. Elisha declared, 'There will be more than enough.' Indeed, they ate and they had some over according to the word of the anointed person.

And it came to pass after this, that Benhadad king of Syria gathered all his host, and went up, and besieged Samaria. And there was a great famine in Samaria: and, behold, they besieged it, until an ass's head was *sold* for fourscore pieces of silver, and the fourth part of a cab of dove's dung for five *pieces* of silver.

And as the king of Israel was passing by upon the wall, there cried a woman unto him, saying, Help, my lord, O king.

And he said, If the LORD do not help thee, whence shall I help thee? Out of the barnfloor, or out of the winepress?

And the king said unto her, what aileth thee? And she answered, this woman said unto me, give thy son, that we may eat him to day, and we will eat my son to morrow.

So we boiled my son, and did eat him: and I said unto her on the next day, Give thy son, that we may eat him: and she hath hid her son.

And it came to pass, when the king heard the words of the woman, that he rent his clothes; and he passed by upon the wall, and the people looked, and, behold, *he had* sackcloth within upon his flesh.

2 Kings 6:24-30

Then Elisha said, Hear ye the word of the LORD; Thus saith the LORD, To morrow about this time *shall* a measure of fine flour *be sold* for a shekel, and two measures of barley for a shekel, in the gate of Samaria.

Then a lord on whose hand the king leaned answered the man of God, and said, Behold, *if* the LORD would make windows in heaven, might this thing be? And he said, Behold, thou shalt see *it* with thine eyes, but shalt not eat thereof.

2 Kings 7:1-2

Our whole lives are made up of the struggle to have enough for our lives. God is the key to your abundance. He has his agents, the anointed ones, through whom God's abundance will come to you. You must open up yourself to these agents of abundance. Your anointed man is your agent of abundance. God will give you more than you carry, more that you can use and more than you will ever need through the anointed person and his anointing. The anointing breaks the yoke and it will break the yoke of lack in your life.

In the day of famine when there was so much hunger that people were eating their own children, Elijah prophesied great abundance. As usual, there were mockers who said, "How can this be possible?" The anointed man, Elisha (carrying the double portion of anointing) said to him, "You will see but you will not enjoy it." It was a prophecy of this officer's death. Because the royal officer mocked at Elisha's predictions, he was trampled upon by the people as they rushed to partake of the abundance that had been released through the anointing of the anointed.

All these stories you have read are the exploits of the anointed. The anointed person is carrying a precious heavenly substance called the anointing. He himself is weak and powerless. It is the anointing in him that works. Anointed people are a strange combination of weakness, humanity and power. This combination must not confuse you. You must grow up quickly to respect the anointed and his anointing. If you do so in time, you will experience the blessing that comes from the anointing.

The anointed is an agent for your prosperity, your healing, your deliverance, your abundance and your miracle. Open yourself to the anointed and his anointing. Be wiser than the royal officer of the king who doubted and ridiculed the word of the Lord that came from the anointed. It is your day to advance quickly into the next level of your calling and ministry. Next year by this time, you will never be found at the same spot again, in Jesus' name. Amen!

CHAPTER 16

The Anointing Creates Your Room

....ye shall receive the gift of the Holy Ghost.

Acts 2:38

The greatest gift ever given to men is the gift of the Holy Ghost. Your great gift is the anointing of the Spirit. Your whole life will be defined by the gift that God pours upon you. Are you not appreciative that when God wanted to give you a gift He gave you Himself – the mighty Spirit of God? What an unspeakable gift! What a precious gift! The four great implications of receiving the gift of the Holy Spirit and the gift of the anointing are outlined in the following marvelous Scriptures.

1. **The anointing creates the room of ministry that you will operate in.**

   A MAN'S GIFT MAKETH ROOM FOR HIM, and bringeth him before great men.

   Proverbs 18:6

The anointing that you have will define your room on this earth. The anointing defines what kind of room you will live in. The anointing defines the quality of the room, the riches of the room, the size of the room of your life and ministry.

Andrae Crouch, whose funeral is being held as I write these words, received a great room of ministry in this world. The world was his parish and his music and ministry spanned across the whole world. There is hardly any Christian today who does not know or sing an Andrae Crouch song. His life could have been confined to a small black community in Los Angeles. But the gift of God made a much bigger room for him.

Andrae Crouch is not famous across the world because of his education. He was dyslexic and therefore not very educated. It was not his colour that made room for him in the whole world. He was a black man and by all standards he should have been rejected by many. It is the gift that made room for him.

If the room of your life is defined by your gift, should it not be your earnest desire and quest to seek for the gift of God? Is it not surprising to you that people spend little time discussing or even seeking the gift of the Holy Spirit? Does it not surprise you that ministers of the gospel rarely ever teach or preach about the gift of the anointing of the Holy Ghost?

2. The anointing promotes you and brings you before greatness.

A man's gift maketh room for him, and BRINGETH HIM BEFORE GREAT MEN.

Proverbs 18:6

Don't you want to go before great men? Have you ever been invited to speak before great men? It is a tragedy to be giftless. When you are giftless you will be roomless. Today will be the last day you will be found giftless in the name of Jesus!

I have stood before people in many different nations in the world not because of my education. I have spoken to Asians, South Americans, Africans and Americans in different nations of the world. It was my gift that carried me to these places. It was my gift that opened the door for me to stand where I stood.

Only a gift can carry you to stand before great men. On the occasion that I have stood before presidents it has not been because of my education, my background or may schooling. It has been because of the gift that God placed on my life.

3. The anointing has been given to profit you.

But the manifestation of the Spirit is given TO EVERY MAN TO PROFIT withal.

1 Corinthian 12:7

The anointing is designed for the body of Christ to profit or benefit from. All necessary benefits of your life are connected to the anointing. It is designed for the people to profit and benefit. An entire congregation can benefit and profit from it.

One of the great manifestations of the Spirit is the gift of being a pastor, an apostle, a teacher and an evangelist. Today, the gift of being a pastor, a teacher and an apostle has been manifested in my life and many others too. It was given also for our profiting. That is why we have profited in the ministry.

Your profiting will also be experienced as the manifestation of the Spirit is poured out on you. God wants you to profit and to be blessed. That is why He pours out His Spirit and His power on you. Do not miss this outstanding blessing – the blessing of the manifestation of the anointing of the Holy Spirit on you! If you have no time to receive the anointing do not be jealous of those who are benefitting from it.

4. The anointing has been given to establish you.

For I long to see you, that I may impart unto you some spiritual gift, to the end ye may be established;

Romans 1:11

The anointing is designed to establish you in whatever you are doing. The anointing is what establishes you in life. Establishment is by the gift that has been given to you. Parents earnestly try to establish their children by giving them gifts of property riches and wealth. When you are established, you cannot be tipped into a crisis by a landlord. When you are established, the events in this life will not move you or destabilize you. Your establishment is caused by the power of God and the gift of God.

Today, you are moving higher! You are moving from being a beginner into being established! You are moving from living on the edge to living in the midst of establishment! Today, you are moving from being on the border of poverty into the level of super abundance and establishment through the gift of God!

Paul said, "I long to see you." I want to impart to you my gift because I know it will establish you. Your great establishment is here because the gift of God is here. Instability comes to an end today because of the gift and the anointing of the Holy Spirit!

CHAPTER 17

The Spices of the Anointing

Oil for the light, spices for anointing oil, and for sweet incense,

Exodus 25:6

And the Lord said unto Moses, Take unto thee sweet spices, stacte, and onycha, and galbanum; these sweet spices with pure frankincense:of each shall there be a like weight:

And thou shalt make it a perfume, a confection after the art of the apothecary, tempered together, pure and holy:

And thou shalt beat some of it very small, and put of it before the testimony in the tabernacle of the congregation, where I will meet with thee:it shall be unto you most holy.

And as for the perfume which thou shalt make, ye shall not make to yourselves according to the composition thereof:it shall be unto thee holy for the LORD.

Whosoever shall make like unto that, to smell thereto, shall even be cut off from his people

Exodus 30:34-38

The spice of the anointing is that which makes the anointing striking, provocative, stimulating and exciting. Once the anointing is spiced it has peculiar noticeable characteristics.

The anointing oil of the Old Testament had a peculiar composition. This peculiar composition was determined by God Himself. These spices would flavour and characterise the oil in a particular, unique way. To spice something is to give the thing zest and to make it interesting. To spice something is to give the thing piquancy. To give something piquancy is to make it stimulating, interesting and attractive. Different anointings carry within them interesting features that are stimulating and attractive.

Within every calling and every gift there are elements which are given for the purpose of making the thing interesting, stimulating and attractive. Most callings and anointings have a number of stimulating and attractive things within them. When Jesus spoke of giving men talents, He described how some were given one, some were given two and some were given ten. All these talents work together to make a person's gifting and anointing stimulating and exciting. It is important to discover the spices of the peculiar anointing that you are dealing with. Your anointing is a peculiar mixture that is God-given and God-determined.

For instance, the teaching anointing of Kenneth Hagin came along with the ability to publish books, produce audio tapes and also to create a Bible School. However, the anointing upon Derek Prince, also a Bible teacher, was the teaching anointing which was made stimulating and attractive by audio tapes and millions of published books. The teaching anointing of Derek Prince was made particularly stimulating and attractive by an analysis on demonology teaching. The teaching anointing on Kenneth Hagin was made stimulating and attractive by special teachings on faith and healing. Fantastic visions of Jesus Christ dotted the teaching anointing that was on Kenneth Hagin making him a world-renowned prophet. The anointing on Benny Hinn was made stimulating and attractive by powerful miracles and amazing manifestations of the Spirit.

The ministries of people who are called "God's Generals" had provocative and stimulating ministries because of certain traits and spices that were in the anointing they received. The teaching anointing of Kathryn Khulman was made attractive by the spice of healing. People would gather outside the hall for hours before the service, seeking to be touched by the anointing. They would travel for miles and wait outside the hall until the doors were opened. Although she just preached as every other person did, the spice of healing changed the impact of her ministry completely.

The teaching ministry of Kenneth Copeland was spiced with an unusual gift for prosperity. Many ministers have risen up with the spice and the grace to preach on prosperity.

It is important to analyse the components and types of spices that God has placed on certain anointings. There are anointings that are spiced and flavoured with certain types of teachings. I know an anointing that is spiced with teachings on church growth, leadership, the anointing and the ministry.

I know another anointing and ministry which is spiced with church planting, church growth and teachings of prosperity. On the other hand, I know of another anointing which is also spiced with church growth and church planting but without any special teaching on prosperity. Some men of God have an anointing to teach which is spiced with singing and music.

Begin to look out and analyse what spices are flowing in the anointing God is leading you to. It is important to tap into these anointings so that you are characterized by certain anointings and flavour. Today, mummies in Egypt which have been excavated are said to contain certain spices which still remain in them. Spices indeed create an unusual characteristic that is striking.

Great Grace Was Upon Them

Paul said to Timothy, "Be strong in the grace which is in Christ Jesus." In other words, be strong in the peculiar grace that is in your calling to Jesus Christ. When the anointing with its peculiar characteristic comes upon you, there is great grace upon your life to do certain things. This great grace is caused by the peculiar and provocative and spicy anointing that is given to you. The great grace to build the church, to have lay people, to have full time people, to go to all the world is upon those who are reading this book right now. The great grace to prosper without teaching and emphasizing on prosperity comes on all who have opened their heart to the blessings of this book. As the grace of God descended upon the apostles, you are now receiving great grace to live your life in obedience to a call rather than in conformity to your traditional upbringing. You will go to lands, nations and places where people with the same family background as yours will never visit. It is great grace that allows a ministry an anointing to have a genuinely international appeal, speaking to French, Spanish, Portuguese, Russian and Indian people. This is the grace that is coming upon you right now. The power of God is unique and makes you do unique things. Today marks the end of your giftless existence. Through the gift of God and through the peculiar spices bestowed in that anointing, you have ascended into a seat reserved only for those who have a great grace upon their lives.

CHAPTER 18

Anointing for Babies and Sucklings

At that time Jesus answered and said, I thank thee, O Father, Lord of heaven and earth, because thou hast hid these things from the wise and prudent, and hast revealed them unto babes.

Matthew 11:25

Why do babes and sucklings get the anointing of the anointed? Because they believe, they copy completely. Grown-ups do not copy completely and grown-ups do not trust fully. There is a great secret in admiring the anointed and his anointing. This is the secret that babes and suckling have, but grown-ups do not have. You cannot receive from somebody you criticize. The secret of genuine admiration is the secret of babes and sucklings.

John, the youngest disciple, was full of admiration for Jesus whom he had seen, looked upon and handled. (1 John 1:1-2). The discourse of John chapter one reveals his admiration of the Jesus he saw being crucified.

Admiration for a man of God is not the same as hero worship or making a man into God. I am not talking about illegally falling in love with the anointed. Genuine admiration is what is found in babes and sucklings.

You can receive the anointing through genuine admiration. Without genuine admiration your mouth is not open enough to receive from the anointed.

Genuine admiration brings you to a place of relaxation, which makes you open to the anointing. Genuine admiration is a key to the special anointings. It is the feeling of the greatness of the person that opens the door of your spirit to receive the anointing from the anointed.

Do not let the enemy tell you that you are in love with the anointed. Do not let enemy ask you, "Is he God?" Remember that the one who admires most is the one who receives most.

And said unto him, hearest thou what these say? And Jesus saith unto them, Yea; have ye never read, Out of the mouth of babes and sucklings thou hast perfected praise?

Matthew 21:16

The highest form of praise is found in babies and sucklings. It is perfected in children. Breast milk contains everything the baby needs. It is sucklings who catch the anointing of the anointed. The suckling latches on the breast because the breast milk is its stew, sausages, orange juice, water, vitamin C, etc. It is in this group that the perfected ultimate Christianity is found.

When you become a suckling of the anointed it means you have attached yourself with one of the breasts of the anointed and you are drawing power and anointing from the anointed. The highest grade of receptivity to the anointing is found in the babes and sucklings.

Overcome the familiarity that does not allow you to genuinely admire the anointed.

But whereunto shall I liken this generation? It is like unto children sitting in the markets, and calling unto their fellows,

And saying, we have piped unto you, and ye have not danced; we have mourned unto you, and ye have not lamented.

For John came neither eating nor drinking, and they say, He hath a devil.

The Son of man came eating and drinking, and they say, Behold a man gluttonous, and a winebibber, a friend of publicans and sinners. But wisdom is justified of her children.

Matthew 11:16-19

Notice why the failures occur with children not dancing or mourning! Note why people did not listen to John the Baptist and how it will happen to you too, but in a different way. Jesus knew they did not dance for John and they would not mourn for Him when the time came.

With a certain attitude, no matter the power or anointing that comes, people do not respond to it. This is the attitude of a vagabond in the market. Nothing impresses or affects him. This is an attitude opposed to the attitude of a babe or suckling. Be careful not to turn into a child that does not respond to greatness around him. John the Baptist came with great power. He was not eating, was fasting all the time, had a sunken look and they said he had a demon.

Jesus came but they did not respond to His eating, drinking and fellowshipping with others.

CHAPTER 19

Accept the Helpers
of the Anointed

And Elisha said, As the Lord of hosts liveth, before whom I stand, surely, were it not that I regard the presence of Jehoshaphat the king of Judah, I would not look toward thee, nor see thee.

But now bring me a minstrel. And it came to pass, when the minstrel played, that the hand of the Lord came upon him.

2 Kings 3:14-15

There are some people who depend on helpers. The greater the anointing on a servant of the Lord, the more help he needs to accomplish his God-given task. Helpers abound where the anointing abounds. The helping grace is similar to the Holy Spirit who is sent to help us. If you cannot accept, relate or deal with helpers you will not do well.

Without the input of the minstrel, the anointing could not have descended upon Elisha for him to prophesy and bring deliverance to Israel. In order to relate to great and anointed men of God, you will have to deal with their Bishops, assistants, secretaries and singers. Throughout my relationship with Dr Cho, the pastor of the largest church in the world, I have had to relate to him through his assistants and those he has chosen to work with.

CHAPTER 20

Travel with the Anointed

And it came to pass, when the Lord would take up Elijah into heaven by a whirlwind, that ELIJAH WENT WITH ELISHA FROM GILGAL.

2 Kings 2:1

And Elijah said unto Elisha, Tarry here, I pray thee; for the Lord hath sent me to Bethel. And Elisha said unto him, As the Lord liveth, and as thy soul liveth, I will not leave thee. So THEY WENT DOWN TO BETHEL.

2 Kings 2:2

And Elijah said unto him, Elisha, tarry here, I pray thee; for the Lord hath sent me to Jericho. And he said, As the Lord liveth, and as thy soul liveth, I will not leave thee. So THEY CAME TO JERICHO.

2 Kings 2:4

And Elijah said unto him, Tarry, I pray thee, here; for the Lord hath sent me to Jordan. And he said, As the Lord liveth, and as thy soul liveth, I will not leave thee. And THEY TWO WENT ON.

2 Kings 2:6

When the disciples lost Judas to treachery, pride, forgetfulness, unforgiveness and disloyalty they had to choose someone else to replace him. Jesus was not around so they had to use a comprehensive system which covered all options for the selection of a successor. That was the system of companying with the anointed and his anointed.

Companying with the anointed and his anointing covers the system of hearing the anointed, seeing the anointed, touching the anointed, the system of drawing the anointed through your obedience.

The Secret of Companying with the Anointed

There is no way you could be of a certain order of the anointing without companying with the anointing.

Men and brethren, this Scripture must needs have been fulfilled, which the Holy Ghost by the mouth of David spake before concerning Judas, which was guide to them that took Jesus.

For he was numbered with us, and had obtained part of this ministry.

Now this man purchased a field with the reward of iniquity; and falling headlong, he burst asunder in the midst, and all his bowels gushed out.

And it was known unto all the dwellers at Jerusalem; insomuch as that field is called in their proper tongue, Aceldama, that is to say, The field of blood.

For it is written in the book of Psalms, Let his habitation be desolate, and let no man dwell therein: and his bishoprick let another take.

Wherefore of these men which have companied with us all the time that the Lord Jesus went in and out among us,

Beginning from the baptism of John, unto that same day that he was taken up from us, must one be ordained to be a witness with us of his resurrection.

And they appointed two, Joseph called Barsabas, who was surnamed Justus, and Matthias.

And they prayed, and said, Thou, Lord, which knowest the hearts of all men, shew whether of these two thou hast chosen, That he may take part of this ministry and apostleship, from which Judas by transgression fell, that he might go to his own place.

Acts 1:16-25

The most anointed prophet ever, Elisha, travelled with his father on different occasions. There made four famous trips which were recorded in the Bible.

1. They travelled together to Gilgal

2. They travelled together from Gilgal to Bethel

3. They travelled together from Bethel to Jericho

4. They travelled together from Jericho to Jordan

It was during one of these journeys that Elisha made the famous request for a double portion of the anointing.

Why is travelling with the anointed important?

The choice of a replacement for Judas Iscariot was made based on someone who had travelled with Jesus Christ to the same extent that the other apostles had. The extent of travelling with the anointed is very important.

Wherefore of these MEN WHICH HAVE COMPANIED WITH US ALL THE TIME THAT THE LORD JESUS WENT IN AND OUT among us, Beginning from the baptism of John, unto that same day that he was taken up from us, must one be ordained to be a witness with us of his resurrection.

Acts 1:21-22

Seven Reasons Why You Must Travel with the Anointed

1. **Travel with the anointed to see how he overcomes hostility.**

   And he went out from thence, and came into his own country; and his disciples follow him. And when the sabbath day was come, he began to teach in the synagogue: and many hearing him were astonished, saying, From whence hath this man these things? and what wisdom is this which is given unto him, that even such mighty works are wrought by his hands? Is not this the carpenter, the son of Mary, the brother of James, and Joses, and of Juda, and Simon? And are not his sisters here with us? And they were offended at him.

   Mark 6:1-3

   On Jesus' trip to Nazareth He encountered great hostilities. If you read the life story of men of God you will realise that they encountered great hostility in certain places. Kenneth Hagin spoke of places in which he was not able to function and operate in the anointing at a certain level. Oral Roberts was highly rejected when he travelled to Melbourne, Australia and had to close his campaign three days before the scheduled time.

2. **Travel with the anointed to see the greatness of his calling.**

   A prophet is not accepted in his own country. When you travel with the anointed you will see his acceptance in the way that you will never see in his own country. You will see the genuineness, openness and acceptance of the gift which you work with. It will minister to you that you are with a greater person than you originally thought. Perhaps this is the greatest reason for travelling with the anointed. Your eyes are opened and you see what God has given to you. Most of the great works of Jesus were done in Chorazin and Bethsaida.

> **Woe unto thee, Chorazin! Woe unto thee, Bethsaida! For if the mighty works, which were done in you, had been done in Tyre and Sidon, they would have repented long ago in sackcloth and ashes.**
>
> **Matthew 11:21**

Jesus did not do great works everywhere. No man of God does the same level of great works everywhere. There are places where he is able to do great works and there are places where he simply cannot function.

3. Travel with the anointed to hear the real explanations of some of his mysterious teachings.

There are many things that Jesus said to His disciples that He did not say in public. There are things He intentionally hid from the public which He revealed only when He was privately moving with the disciples. When you travel with the anointed, you will get to understand his message even better than you think you do.

> **And the disciples came, and said unto him, Why speakest thou unto them in parables? He answered and said unto them, Because it is given unto you to know the mysteries of the kingdom of heaven, but to them it is not given.**
>
> **Matthew 13:10-11**

4. Travel with the anointed to hear teachings that are reserved for only ministers.

If you do not travel with the anointed, you will only hear congregational sermons.

For example, the teaching on marriage that the congregation receives is, "Love your wives; and wives submit to your own husbands." However, there are teachings which Jesus gave about marriage which are reserved for pastors.

Jesus told His disciples;

If any man come to me, and hate not his father, and mother, and wife, and children, and brethren, and sisters, yea, and his own life also, he cannot be my disciple.

Luke 14:26

This Scripture seems to directly contradict the Scripture which says husbands should love their wives. In this case Jesus said, if you do not hate your wife you cannot be my disciple. This teaching about marriage is applicable to people who are called at a higher level and may have to hate their wives in order to fulfil their divine calling. Do you want to hear higher things which are reserved for pastors and ministers? Then you must travel with the anointed. Every time I have travelled with an anointed person, I have experienced the great blessing of great revelations in my life.

5. Travel with the anointed so that you will hear secrets.

When Jesus came into the coasts of Caesarea Philippi, he asked his disciples, saying, Whom do men say that I the Son of man am? And they said, Some say that thou art John the Baptist: some, Elias; and others, Jeremias, or one of the prophets.

He saith unto them, But whom say ye that I am? And Simon Peter answered and said, Thou art the Christ, the Son of the living God.

And Jesus answered and said unto him, Blessed art thou, Simon Barjona: for flesh and blood hath not revealed it unto thee, but my Father which is in heaven. And I say also unto thee, That thou art Peter, and upon this rock I will build my church; and the gates of hell shall not prevail against it.

Matthew 16:13-18

On Jesus' journey to Caesarea Philippi, He revealed the secret of who he really was to the disciples. When you travel with the anointed, you instantly become part of an elite or special group. This newborn specialness entitles you to secrets and privileges that a few enjoy. It is almost automatic that someone who journeys with you will hear things that few will ever hear. Indeed, to travel with the anointed is one of the privileges and doors of access one can have.

6. Travel with the anointed so that you can dine with him.

So when they had finished breakfast, Jesus said to Simon Peter, "Simon, son of John, do you love Me more than these?" He said to Him, "Yes, Lord; You know that I love You." He said to him, "Tend My lambs."

John 21:15 (NASB)

Perhaps eating provides an environment in which a peculiar aspect of the anointing begins to function. You will recall that some of the most powerful things that concerned Jesus Christ were spoken when the disciples were at table. These revelations came when they were eating and not when they were fasting.

Holy Communion which marks our Christianity was ministered at the last supper that Jesus had with His disciples. It was called the last supper because there were many suppers of which that was the last.

Jesus' famous visits to rich people's homes were over food. When He told Peter, "If you love me feed my sheep", it was another discussion over a meal.

7. Travel with the anointed because certain events are prophetically determined to take place at certain physical locations.

And, being assembled together with them, commanded them that they should NOT DEPART FROM

JERUSALEM, but wait for the promise of the Father, which, saith he, ye have heard of me.

Acts 1:4

Even though the disciples scattered to Galilee, Jesus asked them to go back to Jerusalem and wait there for the Holy Spirit. When He was about to be crucified, He moved away from His usual ministry route and headed for Jerusalem. There are certain places where certain things are destined to take place. Perhaps God has determined to pour His Spirit upon you and anoint you at certain meetings, certain places and on certain journeys. Your lack of interest in walking or journeying with the anointed can deprive you of that experience on that journey. Perhaps you just want to travel for a funeral or a wedding but not in order to receive the anointing of the anointed.

CHAPTER 21

How You Can Change Your Anointing Levels

And there appeared unto them cloven tongues like as of fire, and it sat upon each of them. And they were all filled with the Holy Ghost, and began to speak with other tongues, as the Spirit gave them utterance.

Acts 2:3-4

Peter, the apostle was transformed into a powerful preaching apostle who was able to lead thousands of people to great conviction and repentance. You must remember that Jesus had breathed on Peter a few days earlier and he had already received the Holy Spirit. "Then said Jesus to them again, Peace be unto you: as my Father hath sent me, even so send I you. And when he had said this, he breathed on them, and saith unto them, Receive ye the Holy Ghost" (John 20:21-22).

The change in anointing levels suddenly transformed Peter's life. There is a change in the anointing level that will transform you from a weakling into a bold minister. This is the anointing that fell on the day of Pentecost, transforming Peter and others into bold ministers of the gospel. The people were astonished when they saw the effect that the change in the anointing level had made on Peter's life.

The story of Pentecost shows us three wonderful keys that will bring about a change of anointing levels for anyone who cares to receive it.

1. A conviction will lead to a change in anointing levels.

Now when they heard this, they were PRICKED IN THEIR HEART, and said unto Peter and to the rest of the apostles, Men and brethren, what shall we do?

Acts 2:37

"Convictionless" people cannot receive the anointing. The crowds who heard Peter preaching were "pricked in their hearts." This means that they were convicted about what they heard.

Many people are not convicted in their hearts about the importance of the anointing. I know deep down in my heart that there is nothing about me that can make anything work, except the anointing. It is a deep conviction I have that makes me keep searching and speaking about the anointing. Most people do not believe that the anointing is really what is working. Many people think in their hearts, "He is just lucky." Many people think to themselves, "It is because he is American, that's why his ministry is successful." Many people think; "Oh he has a lot of money, that is why it is working for him."

2. Asking questions will lead you to a change in anointing levels.

Now when they heard this, they were pricked in their heart, and said unto Peter and to the rest of the apostles, Men and brethren, WHAT SHALL WE DO?

Acts 2:37

Anointing comes when you start asking questions – when you ask about solutions to real problems that you want to solve.

"Men and brethren what shall we do?" Most pastors do not ask these questions. When you are in Bible School, you often do not ask certain questions. Going out onto the mission field and doing the work in reality will bring up certain questions. As you begin asking yourself the right questions, you will be led to the anointing. It is almost impossible to make someone who is not thirsty drink water. It is thirst, hunger, that drives a person to seek for the water that he needs. Young and presumptuous people who assume that they can do everything are filled with useless pride and never ask the right questions.

When I began my church, I really wanted to know how to make the church grow. I wanted to know how I could heal the sick. I wanted to know how Kathryn Khulman and Benny Hinn became as anointed as they were. When I began to ask the right questions about the ministry, I began progressing towards a higher anointing level.

Asking foolish questions will not lead you to the anointing. Many people ask foolish questions like, "Where do you live? What car do you drive? Don't you ever get tired?" These are foolish questions because they have no bearing on the anointing. Others also ask questions like, "How are you able to maintain your zeal all these years? How are you able to write the books you do? How are you able to combine the ministry with other aspects of life?" You see, the answers to these questions can be the contents of an entire four hundred-page book. How are you expected to genuinely answer these questions in one minute?

Instead of asking interview questions to just make a person speak to cover the time, you must in your heart ask genuine questions that will help your spiritual life to develop. The answers to the questions should open you up to the anointing.

A foolish question is also a question whose answer you are not really interested in. Why are you asking questions that you are not really interested in? People ask me questions about the things that I have already written about. When I point to the books they lose interest. This means they were not really interested in getting an answer to their question.

3. **A change of mind will lead to a change of anointing levels.**

> **Then Peter said unto them, REPENT, and be baptized every one of you in the name of Jesus Christ for the remission of sins, and ye shall receive the gift of the Holy Ghost.**

> **Acts 2:38**

A change of mind is necessary if you are to receive a change of anointing levels. Peter asked the people to repent so that they could receive the Holy Ghost. Without repentance you cannot receive the power of the Holy Ghost.

Repentance speaks of a change of mind. Repentance speaks of a new way of thinking. As you turn around in the way you think and believe, you will discover a change in the level of anointing.

CHAPTER 22

What It Means to be an Anointed Servant

Behold my servant, whom I uphold; mine elect, in whom my soul delighteth; I have put my spirit upon him: he shall bring forth judgment to the Gentiles.

He shall not cry, nor lift up, nor cause his voice to be heard in the street.

A bruised reed shall he not break, and the smoking flax shall he not quench: he shall bring forth judgment unto truth.

He shall not fail nor be discouraged, till he have set judgment in the earth: and the isles shall wait for his law.

Isaiah 42:1-4

There is a special anointing on the servant of God in whom God delights. May this anointing be upon you! The prophet Isaiah spoke of this anointed servant on whom the Spirit of God would rest. He would have certain characteristics. May these characteristics always be found on you after today! This is the last day that you will be found without the gift of the spirit. Many desire to be servants of God because there is a difference between he that serveth God and he that serveth Him not. Even higher than that is the opportunity to be an anointed servant. This will be your story and your testimony from today onwards. As you read these qualities of the anointed servant as prophesied by Isaiah, they are coming upon you to stay. Amen!

1. The anointing of the anointed servant will cause you to be a delight to the one who chose you.

   Behold my servant, whom I uphold; mine elect, IN WHOM MY SOUL DELIGHTETH; I have put my spirit upon him: he shall bring forth judgment to the Gentiles.

   Isaiah 42:1

2. The anointing of the anointed servant will open your ministry up to the Gentiles and you will walk in the anointing of the anointed servant.

   Behold my servant, whom I uphold; mine elect, in whom my soul delighteth; I have put my spirit upon him: HE SHALL BRING FORTH JUDGMENT TO THE GENTILES.

   Isaiah 42:1

3. The anointing of the anointed servant will cause you to trust in the anointing and you not to strain or stretch yourself in the natural.

   HE SHALL NOT CRY, NOR LIFT UP, nor cause his voice to be heard in the street.

   Isaiah 42:2

4. The anointing of the anointed servant will cause you not to waste your ministerial energy on useless activities that are not part of your calling. This is what is meant by "His voice will not be heard on the streets".

He shall not cry, nor lift up, nor cause HIS VOICE TO BE HEARD IN THE STREET.

Isaiah 42:2

5. The anointing of the anointed servant will cause you to bring healing to broken people.

A BRUISED REED SHALL HE NOT BREAK, and the smoking flax shall he not quench: he shall bring forth judgment unto truth.

Isaiah 42:3

6. The anointing of the anointed servant will cause you to help failing and dying ministries.

A bruised reed shall he not break, and THE SMOKING FLAX SHALL HE NOT QUENCH: he shall bring forth judgment unto truth.

Isaiah 42:3

7. The anointing of the anointed servant will enable you to preach the truth even when it is hard and unpopular.

A bruised reed shall he not break, and the smoking flax shall he not quench: HE SHALL BRING FORTH JUDGMENT UNTO TRUTH.

Isaiah 42:3

8. The anointing of the anointed servant will cause you never to fail.

HE SHALL NOT FAIL nor be discouraged, till he have set judgment in the earth: and the isles shall wait for his law.

Isaiah 42:4

9. The anointing of the anointed servant will cause you to overcome discouragement.

   He shall not fail NOR BE DISCOURAGED, till he have set judgment in the earth: and the isles shall wait for his law.

   Isaiah 42:4

10. The anointing of the anointed servant will cause your message to be relevant in distant islands.

    He shall not fail nor be discouraged, till he have set judgment in the earth: and THE ISLES SHALL WAIT FOR HIS LAW.

    Isaiah 42:4

CHAPTER 23

Boldness: The Final Step to the Anointing

Let us therefore come boldly unto the throne of grace, that we may obtain mercy, and find grace to help in time of need.

Hebrews 4:16

ll steps to the anointing are useless without boldness. Without the boldness you stand outside the Holy Place which contains the anointing.

Steps to the Anointing in the Tabernacle

The laver, incense, shewbread, candle are in vain without boldness!

Step No.1: The courtyard

Step No. 2: The altar of sacrifice

Step No. 3: The laver

Step No. 4: The shewbread

Step No. 5: The candlestick

Step No. 6: The incense

Step No. 7: Boldness to enter the Holy of Holies where the anointing dwells.

Four Types of Boldness

1. The boldness of faith declarations.

Declare the impossible. Declare the unbelievable. Declare the great things only God can do.

We having the same spirit of faith, according as it is written, I believed, and therefore have I spoken; we also believe, and therefore speak;

2 Corinthians 4:13

2. The boldness of obedience under the threat of danger.

Then Esther bade them return Mordecai this answer, Go, gather together all the Jews that are present in Shushan, and fast ye for me, and neither eat nor drink three days,

115

night or day: I also and my maidens will fast likewise; and so will I go in unto the king, which is not according to the law: and if I perish, I perish.

Esther 4:15-16

3. The boldness towards new things in the face of traditional people.

Behold, the former things are come to pass, and new things do I declare: before they spring forth I tell you of them.

Isaiah 42:9

4. ⁷⁷The boldness of great projects under the threat of shame and failure.

But it came to pass, that when Sanballat heard that we builded the wall, he was wroth, and took great indignation, and mocked the Jews. And he spake before his brethren and the army of Samaria, and said, What do these feeble Jews? will they fortify themselves? will they sacrifice? will they make an end in a day? will they revive the stones out of the heaps of the rubbish which are burned? Now Tobiah the Ammonite was by him, and he said, Even that which they build, if a fox go up, he shall even break down their stone wall.

Hear, O our God; for we are despised: and turn their reproach upon their own head, and give them for a prey in the land of captivity: And cover not their iniquity, and let not their sin be blotted out from before thee: for they have provoked thee to anger before the builders. So built we the wall; and all the wall was joined together unto the half thereof: for the people had a mind to work.

Nehemiah 4:1-6